Hamlyn Colour Guides

Amphibians
and Reptiles

Hamlyn Colour Guides
Amphibians
and Reptiles

by Václav Laňka and Zbyšek Vít

Illustrated by
Libuše and Jaromír Knotek

HAMLYN

Translated by Margot Schierlová
Graphic design by Jaromír Knotek
Designed and produced by Artia for
Hamlyn Publishing,
a division of The Hamlyn Publishing Group Limited,
Bridge House, London Road, Twickenham, Middlesex, England

ISBN 0 600 30571 6
Printed in Czechoslovakia
3/15/12/51-02

CONTENTS

AMPHIBIAN CHARACTERISTICS

Amphibians (class Amphibia) form an intermediate stage between aquatic and completely terrestrial vertebrates and were the first vertebrates to become adapted to life on dry land. This class of animals shows great diversity of form. If the appearance of extinct forms is also taken into account, the general basic shape of the body of terrestrial vertebrates can be seen to have developed from that of tailed amphibians (Urodela). Limbless amphibians (Apoda) and tailless amphibians (Anura) are derived forms.

In common with any large group of animals, the amphibians cannot be characterized by a single description applying to all the members. There are, however, basic characters common to most of the species, and absence or modification of these is exceptional.

The word 'first' occurs a number of times in connection with amphibians. They were the first vertebrates to develop paired limbs capable of locomotion on dry ground, the first to have auditory ossicles and a middle ear and to have a sensory organ, the vomeronasal organ (which will be discussed in connection with reptiles), localized on the palate in the oral cavity. The eyes were protected for the first time by eyelids and lacrimal glands and ducts appeared for the first time.

Amphibians are ectothermic, their body temperature varying with and being dependent upon the temperature of the environment. Although they were the first vertebrates to acquire paired limbs adapted for locomotion on dry ground, their limbs are variously modified or reduced. Amphibians have soft, moist, richly vascularized skin which plays an important role in respiration. The skin is smooth and has only a thin horny layer, which peels off from time to time. Scattered in the deep layers of the skin are groups of finely branching pigment cells called chromatophores. These contain several types of pigment, from black melanin to yellow and red lipochrome, and sometimes guanine crystals, which give the skin a metallic lustre. Some amphibians are able to change colour. This involves shifts and recombinations of the fine pigment particles and it is brought about by external factors (temperature, humidity, light) and by changes in the state of the animal's nervous system. Large numbers of poison and mucous glands are also present in the skin. The mucous glands are distributed evenly over the body and keep the surface of the skin moist. The large poison glands contain active irritant secretions and toxins. These are defence weapons and are used to deter would-be attackers. The skin and the mucous membrane of the buccol (mouth) cavity with their rich network of blood capillaries, allow oxygen to be absorbed directly from both air and water. Cutaneous respiration is

Fig. 1. Representatives of the main groups of amphibians: a — limbless amphibian (order Apoda, genus *Ichthyophis*), b — tailless amphibian (order Anura, genus *Rana*), c — tailed amphibian (order Urodela, genus *Salamandra*).

very effective and during hibernation it is responsible for the total oxygen requirements of the animal.

Amphibians have a partially cartilaginous skeleton, there are no opercula on the skull and the branchial apparatus itself is reduced. Amphibians were also the first vertebrates in which an auditory ossicle (or ossicles) developed. These animals have a wide gape and they have tiny teeth on the roof of the mouth and in the jaws. Amphibians are mostly unable to bite or chew, however, and can only seize their food and help it into their gullet. The ducts of the organs of reproduction and elimination open into a common passage — the cloaca.

The amphibian heart has two separate auricles and a single ventricle, the latter containing fibres which partially prevent the arterial and venous blood from blending.

Amphibian eggs are surrounded by a jelly-like membrane and develop in water. The larvae likewise develop in water, respire by means of gills and undergo metamorphosis. The adult animals are generally adapted to at least a temporary life on dry land and breathe by means of lungs.

Metamorphosis is a characteristic feature of the life cycle of amphibians. It comprises a series of developmental changes during which the larval organism gradually becomes an adult organism. The whole process is regulated by the thyroid hormone. Many amphibian larvae are very different from their parents. They have a different appearance, a different method of respiration and a different vascular, alimentary and locomotive system. During metamorphosis many organs are completely reconstructed (formation of the mouth is completed, the intestine shortens), disappear altogether (the tail, the gills, the suction organ), or are formed as completely new structures (the limbs, the lungs, the auditory organs).

Occasionally the larva is unable to complete its metamorphosis and is obliged to hibernate in the larval state. In this event metamorphosis takes place after hibernation. Sometimes, however, the larva loses its capacity for transformation altogether, and goes on living as a larva. It can actually attain sexual maturity and reproduce in the larval form — a phenomenon known as neoteny. Some neotenic larvae can be induced to undergo metamorphosis by feeding them on thyroid tissue, or by adding thyroid hormone to their food.

AMPHIBIANS AT CLOSE QUARTERS

Amphibians primarily inhabit damp ground in the most diverse parts of the world. They never live in totally arid deserts, in the sea or in the polar regions. Today 2,300 species of amphibians are known, divided into three very clearly defined orders. The orders in turn are divided into a total of 21 families with a large number of genera. Let us now take a close look at the three orders and see how they differ from the basic pattern, examine their specific features and find in what ways they differ from one another. In the characterization of the various orders mention will also be made of the typical features of chosen large genera, representatives of which are illustrated in this book.

Limbless amphibians, caecilians (Order Apoda)

This order has just one family, the members of which are distributed in South America, tropical Africa and Asia. Caecilians are the most primitive amphibians, but they form a highly specialized group. Only recent forms are known, for no fossil finds are available. These animals have a long, wormlike body with a short tail and no limbs or limb-girdles. Their skin is externally segmented, giving them the appearance of annelid worms. Their antiquity is evidenced by the presence in their skin of small chalky lamellae reminiscent of the armour plating of the long extinct amphibians of the order Stegocephala. They have a massive, thick-boned skull, but have no middle ear. Their eyes are covered with skin, an adaptation to their subterranean mode of life. The length of the body has resulted in degeneration of the left half of the lungs (as in snakes). The males have a protrusible copulatory organ. Caecilians can measure from 17 to 135 cm, according to the species. They live in very damp soil, like earthworms, for which they are often mistaken, but unlike earthworms they are carnivorous. The females of some species lay large eggs, rich in yolk, in holes in the ground, while others produce living young. If oviparous, they often coil their body round the eggs and look after them until the young are hatched.

Tailed amphibians (Order Urodela)

This group is divided into eight families with about 22 species. Its members, the salamanders and newts, are distributed over the whole of the globe, with the exception of tropical Africa, Australia and the polar regions. Adult tailed amphibians have an elongate body and two pairs of approximately equally developed limbs. In the vast majority of species there are four clawless digits on the forelimbs and five on the hind limbs. Some species have severely or completely reduced limbs. The tail is retained in adulthood. The skeleton contains a large number of vertebrae and is partly ossified, and some bones, such as the ribs, have degenerated. Tiny teeth are present on the jaws and palate. The skin is naked and in terrestrial forms it is liberally supplied with glands. Some of the mucous glands have been converted to poison glands — in the genus *Salamandra,* for instance, there are prominent poison glands behind the eyes. Salamanders and newts shed their skin in one piece.

The skin plays an important role in respiration, indeed the lungless salamanders of the genus *Spelerpes* and other species of the Plethodontidae breathe only through their skin. Otherwise, adult salamanders breathe with paired, elongate lung sacs with a smooth inner wall, which, in water, also act as a hydrostatic organ, like the swim bladder of a fish. Salamander and newt larvae breathe by means of richly vascularized external feathery gills, which generally gradually grow smaller and smaller and finally disappear as metamorphosis is completed. In many permanently aquatic species, however, internal and/or external gills persist throughout the whole of the animal's life. The Olm, for instance, has both types of gills.

Tailed amphibians have no vocal organs, but some species are able to inflate themselves with air and to let it out again to the accompaniment of faint whistling sounds. The auditory apparatus of tailed amphibians lacks a middle ear and an eardrum. The eyes have movable lids. In specialized groups like olms, for example, adult individuals have only rudimentary eyes and the function of orientation is taken over mainly by sensory receptors on the surface of the skin. These are the equivalent of the lateral line of fishes, although in amphibians they never actually form a line. The larvae have similar receptors.

The locomotive apparatus of salamanders and newts is adapted in the majority of cases for a life both in water and on dry land. The animals' movements are generally slow and hesitant, but the Caucasus Salamander is as quick and nimble as a lizard, even on land. Tailed amphibians living permanently in water, newts during their aquatic phase and, of course, the larvae, move skilfully under water, with undulating movements of their body and without using their limbs. When swimming they are helped by a more or less well-developed fin-like structure. This is a border of skin which, unlike that of fishes, is not reinforced by bony rays. Most newts develop such a fin during the breeding season, as a secondary sexual characteristic, and in males it is very conspicuous, brightly coloured and sometimes notched. Often it begins on the head and extends dorsally the entire length of the body, right to the tip of the tail, and is usually also developed on the underside of the tail as well. When breeding is over, the fin is resorbed. Females have a less conspicuous fin. Some species, such as the Palmate Newt have webbed toes.

Tailed amphibians are noted for their ability to replace damaged parts of their body by regeneration. If they lose a limb, their tail or even their cornea, it grows again. Another remarkable characteristic is their marked tendency to neoteny and retention of the gills. Neoteny has actually resulted in the formation of whole families — Sirenidae, Proteidae, Amphiumidae — but this happened long ago and metamorphosis cannot even be induced experimentally.

The association of tailed amphibians with water varies from species to species. Some are permanently aquatic (e. g. olms), while others, such as newts, are seasonally aquatic. Others again, like the Fire Salamander, are largely terrestrial, but deposit their larvae or eggs in water. Lastly, there are certain species, such as the Alpine Salamander, which need no more than slight moisture in the soil and do not require water for their eggs or for their larvae, since the latter develop within the body of the female. The seasonal forms have two phases. The aquatic phase is characterized by sexual dimorphism (the males have impressive, brightly coloured fins) and both sexes live in the water. When the breeding season is over, both males and females return to dry land and remain there until the next breeding season.

During the terrestrial phase the differences between the sexes are not evident. Tailed amphibians are usually nocturnal. Adults and fully-grown larvae are carnivorous.

Tailless amphibians (Order Anura)

Frogs and toads are evolutionarily the most advanced of the amphibians. This order is also the largest, since it comprises about 2,000 species divided into twelve families. Frogs and toads have a short body, their spine is composed of a constant number of vertebrae (nine) and their caudal vertebrae have united to form a sword-shaped coccyx known in this case as a urostyle. They have a light, wide skull formed partly of bone and partly of cartilage. In most families there are tiny teeth in the roof of the mouth and in the upper jaw. The lower jaw is toothless. Adult individuals are tailless. Larvae possess a tail but begin to resorb it when the limbs appear. Of the two pairs of limbs, the forelimbs are usually short and have four digits, while the hind limbs are longer and have five digits. The long, powerful hind limbs of the genus *Rana* are perfectly adapted for leaping. The skin is naked and from time to time the outer layer — the epidermis — is shed in strips. The poison glands (e. g. the parotoid glands in toads) often project noticeably beyond the contours of the body. Horny

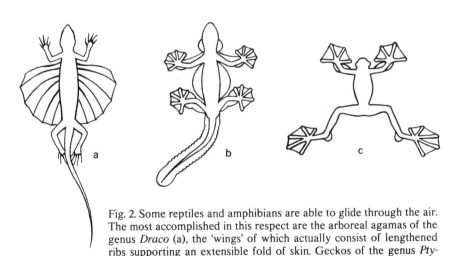

Fig. 2. Some reptiles and amphibians are able to glide through the air. The most accomplished in this respect are the arboreal agamas of the genus *Draco* (a), the 'wings' of which actually consist of lengthened ribs supporting an extensible fold of skin. Geckos of the genus *Ptychozoon* (b) have free flaps and frills of skin on the sides of their head, body and tail, on their limbs and between their toes. Some frogs of the genus *Rhacophorus* (c) use the wide webbing between their toes for gliding.

11

structures derived from the skin are sometimes formed, such as the tubercles which feature on the digits of the males during the breeding season or the claws on the toes of the African Clawed Toad (*Xenopus*). Only the larvae (tadpoles) have fin-like structures. Frogs and toads have webbed feet. This is especially noticeable on their hind limbs, where the webbing plays an important role in swimming. The membrane on the large webbed feet of the tropical 'flying frogs' of the family Rhacophoridae enables these treefrogs to glide through the air (Fig. 2). The skin of frogs and toads is attached to the subcutaneous musculature in narrow strips and the intervening spaces are filled with lymph. This is of great significance for respiration. In the true frogs the skin is responsible for two-thirds to three-quarters of all gaseous exchange. As in the case of the preceding order, it provides the entire oxygen requirements of the animal during hibernation.

Adult frogs and toads also breathe by means of lung sacs, which are paired, internally ciliated organs. At first, the larvae breathe by means of feathery external gills. Later these become covered by a fold of skin and they atrophy. Their place is taken by internal gills, with which the larva breathes until metamorphosis takes place, when they grow steadily smaller and eventually disappear. Their function is taken over by the lung sacs, which have meanwhile had time to develop. The vocal organs are associated with the organs of respiration. The most familiar sound is the voice of the male frogs, which is the dominant sound near lakes and ponds on summer evenings and can usually be heard over a distance of several kilometres. Aquatic species of true frogs, such as the Marsh Frog, have a particularly powerful voice. Behind the corners of their mouth, green frogs have large resonators which can be inflated to form large bladders which amplify the sound formed in the slit-like vocal spaces. Treefrogs (*Hyla*) and toads *(Bufo)* have a single resonator on their throat. Brown frogs have only a subcutaneous resonator, which is localized in the submandibular lymph sac and emits only faint sounds. Spadefoot toads (*Pelobates*) utter curious squeaking sounds. For anurans the voice is an important means of communication during the breeding season. Frogs and toads have well-developed senses of smell and sight. Their eyes are covered with movable lids (each eye has three). The eyes often stand out prominently above the head, thereby facilitating exact estimation of leaping distances. Their position also enables the frog to submerge itself almost completely in water, leaving only its eyes and nostrils showing above the surface — a fact of considerable importance for the safety of the animal. The auditory organs of adult frogs include a middle ear and an eardrum, but the larvae have only sensory receptors, similar to the lateral line receptors of fishes, on the surface of their skin.

Frogs and toads are adapted for locomotion both on land and in water. On the ground they leap or run, but treefrogs have sticky pads at the tip of their toes enabling them to climb plants and cling to the leaves. The way in which frogs swim is also of interest, since for aquatic or semiaquatic vertebrates it is completely atypical. They swim with their hind limbs, keeping their forelimbs close to the chest, and their technique is an example of biologically successful specialization.

Frogs are not all equally dependent upon water. Many species, such as aquatic true frogs, hardly move away from the water at all, while others roam long distances from it and return only to breed. There are, however, exceptions, where reproduction can be achieved away from actual water. For instance, the female *Pipa americana* carries its offspring in fluid-filled chambers formed in the skin on its back, while the young of the Australian toad *Rheobatrachus silus* develop in the stomach of the female.

Frogs and toads are distributed over the greater part of the globe and are the only amphibians to have 'gone up in the world' to inhabit shrubs and trees. They feed on insects and insect larvae and the tadpoles help to remove dead vegetable and animal matter floating in the water.

REPTILIAN CHARACTERISTICS

Reptiles (Reptilia) are fully adapted to life on dry land. Their lack of dependence upon water can be seen from the anatomical structure of various organs and from the specific ways in which the eggs and embryos develop. Consequently, the word 'first' will also be used several times in connection with reptiles.

Reptiles were the first vertebrates to be equipped with a dry, scaly skin protecting their body and preventing it from becoming desiccated. They were the first vertebrates to acquire a distinct cervical spine and a more or less closed thorax. They were likewise the first to develop intercostal muscles of respiration, true kidneys and twelve cranial nerves. For the first time a hard palate was formed at the base of the skull. Accommodation (the ability to focus the eye) was made possible by changes in the shape of the lens. Reptiles never respire by means of gills — not even as developing embryos. Lastly, during reptilian evolution, their embryos developed for the first time in specific embryonal organs — the embryonal membranes.

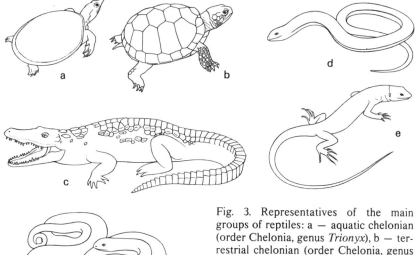

Fig. 3. Representatives of the main groups of reptiles: a — aquatic chelonian (order Chelonia, genus *Trionyx*), b — terrestrial chelonian (order Chelonia, genus *Testudo*), c — crocodile (order Crocodilia, genus *Crocodylus*), d — legless lizard (suborder Sauria, genus *Ophisaurus*), e — true lizard (suborder Sauria, genus *Lacerta*), f — snake (suborder Serpentes, genus *Malpolon*).

Reptiles generally have an elongate, lizard-like body and four limbs, although some groups show a tendency to reduction of the limbs, especially the forelimbs. The evolution of a serpentine body is accompanied by the complete disappearance of the limbs. The reptilian integument gives them protection against desiccation. Their skin is dry and generally devoid of glands, while scales, scutes and shells are characteristic attributes. As in amphibians, the lower layers of the skin contain large numbers of chromatophores. The upper layer (the epidermis) is shed at more or less regular intervals, determined by the age and condition of the animal and the season, and controlled by the thyroid gland. The young shed their skin more often than adults, as they progressively increase in size. To allow the old skin to be shed completely, it is necessary to aid the process by allowing fluid to penetrate between the old epidermis on top and the new epidermis underneath. Water infiltrates between the two layers from external sources through the hygroscopic outer layer of the epidermis. Consequently, when shedding their skin, reptiles look for a damp spot or take a bath. They remove the detached outer layer by rubbing against stones or pieces of rough wood or by crawling through narrow spaces, using their snout and limbs as auxiliary tools.

Reptiles have an almost completely ossified skeleton. The spine is divided into several segments (cervical, thoracic, lumbar, sacral and caudal), the cervical region having the most vertebrae. For the first time the first two vertebrae have a characteristic construction. One (the atlas) has no centrum and only a single articular groove, while the other (the axis) has a tooth-like projection (the odontoid process) on which the atlas (and with it the head) rotates. The skull articulates with the atlas by means of a single occipital joint and can therefore be moved in all directions (unlike the amphibian skull where there are two occipital joints and the head can be moved only up and down). The cranial bones are more ossified than in amphibians. During evolution, the skull became reduced in a manner which provides the key to an understanding of the reptilian zoological system and of the evolution of the mammalian and avian skulls. The well-developed ribs articulate with the vertebrae and form a thorax. In some groups the ribs participate in locomotion, or allow the body to change shape. Reptiles either have fully-developed limbs or the limbs have variously degenerated. Animals which can run well have long limbs with well-developed toes.

As already mentioned, no reptile respires by means of gills and they all possess properly developed paired lungs. Quite often, finger-like sacs containing no respiratory tissue project from the lungs. These are used for inflating the body or as a store for air reserves, or they may participate in the emission of sounds. The vascular system is characterized by division of the heart into a ventricular (arterial) half and an atrial (venous) half. The auricles are entirely separate, but the ventricle is never fully divided. Reptiles were the first animals to have a metanephric kidney. The urinary, reproductive and alimentary organs have a common opening, the cloaca, as in amphibians.

Reptiles have a well-developed sense of smell and often good vision. Their eyes are generally better developed than those of amphibians. They have a large number of sensory cells, three well-developed lids and a lens which achieves accommodation by changing its shape. The auditory apparatus — in particular the part concerned with balance — shows progressive development. Most reptiles (except chelonians) have well-formed teeth on their jaws and palate. These teeth are never used for biting and chewing, however, but for catching and gripping prey. The sexes are separate and the males always have a penis. Many species exhibit sexual dimorphism in the form of differences in colouring, size and the presence or absence of cutaneous outgrowths in males and females. Some species are oviparous, other give birth to live young. The eggs are always laid on land, the female often burying them in the soil. The egg has a protective shell, and inside this the embryo is wrapped in the embryonic membrane, enabling it to develop in its own aquatic environment. The embryo has its own food supply in the yolk sac. These fundamental adaptations permit a completely terrestrial mode of life. The embryos develop directly, without metamorphosis, and the young resemble the adult animals.

Reptiles have a variable body temperature, but are to some extent able to keep it higher than the environmental temperature. Most reptiles are carnivorous, but the diet varies considerably from species to species.

REPTILES AT CLOSE QUARTERS

Reptiles are found all over the world, except in the coldest areas, and they include terrestrial, subterranean, arboreal, amphibian and aquatic species. Today, there are no flying reptiles but in the Mesozoic Era reptiles were also lords of the air. During their evolution various groups of reptiles several times colonized the sea and some species of chelonians and snakes still have a dependence upon it. Reptiles are present in significant numbers only in the tropical, and to some extent, the subtropical, regions. In dry (especially desert and semidesert) areas they are often the most abundant vertebrates.

Reptiles were the ancestral group from which birds and possibly mammals evolved. The wealth of fossil evidence makes their classification relatively easy. They are divided into four orders comprising a total of 47 families with about 5,500 living species.

Turtles and tortoises (Order Chelonia)

This very ancient order has undergone few evolutionary changes from the Permian period down to the present day. Chelonians differ widely in appearance from other reptiles. Their short body is generally domed, although it may be flattened in aquatic species. The short trunk lies in a thick bony shell composed dorsally of a carapace and ventrally of a plastron. The two parts are fused along the sides, leaving a wide free space in front for the head and forelimbs and another one behind for the tail and hind limbs. The shell is constructed of bony plates formed in the skin, which are connected to the widened vertebral spines, ribs, sternum and collarbones. In some species, such as those of the family Trionychidae, the bony shell is covered with horny scutes and plates. The shell may be more or less reduced (e.g. in marine turtles). The legs can be retracted into the shell for protection. The neck and head can often be withdrawn inside it S-wise, or be laid sideways along the body, but in some species it cannot be retracted at all. Chelonians have strong legs adapted for locomotion either on land or in water. Tortoises' legs have long claws and rough scutes and are adapted for walking. Aquatic species have webbed feet (Chelydridae, Emydidae) or very long, flat flippers (Cheloniidae). Chelonians have a solid skull. They have no teeth, but their sharp-edged jaws cut their food efficiently. The skin is dry, and in some species, scent glands are present in the anal region. The epidermis of the limbs, neck and head is shed at regular intervals and from time to time the horny scutes on the shell peel off irregularly. Chelonians breathe by means of lungs, but freshwater and marine species (terrapins and turtles) have developed accessory respiratory organs. These are paired anal sacs situated in front of the opening of the cloaca. These have a rich capillary network the walls of which absorb oxygen from the water. In the case of freshwater terrapins hibernating below the surface, the anal sacs provide the animal with its entire oxygen supply. The existence of this apparatus can be verified by lifting a terrapin out of the water and seeing the large amount of water expelled from its cloaca. Chelonians are carnivorous or omnivorous. These reptiles do not give birth to live young, and always lay their eggs on land. More than a year may elapse between the laying and the hatching of the eggs. Chelonians are divided into twelve families:

Tuataras (Order Rhynchocephalia)

These are primitive terrestrial reptiles with a strongly-built skull and a relatively well-developed single, median, parietal eye, which is an eye-like structure capable of distinguishing light and darkness. The skeleton is very primitive. The spine is composed of biconcave vertebrae and there are transverse uncinate (hooked) processes on the ribs. Tuataras have a lizard-like appearance and may be up to 75 cm. Species almost identical with the present-day Tuatara were living in the Triassic period and were thus contemporaries of the dinosaurs. The Tuatara (or Sphenodon) is rightly looked upon as a living fossil. Only one species — *Sphenodon punctatus* — in a single family, Sphenodontidae, has survived into recent times. This species lives on a few islands to the east and south of New Zealand. Tuataras are predacious nocturnal animals, which spend the day hidden in a hole in the ground. The young hatch out a year after the eggs have been laid.

Scaly reptiles (Order Squamata)

Most of the members of this order have an elongate body covered with a fine scaly skin. The males always have a paired copulatory organ. The majority are terrestrial and phylogenetically very advanced reptiles. There are many articulations on the skull, making the bones easily movable. Among the senses, that of smell is well developed. When the forked tongue is thrust out, it collects samples of near-by odours and when drawn in it passes over a depression in the palate containing olfactory receptors, which is known as the vomeronasal organ or organ of Jacobson and plays an important role in the search for food. Scaly reptiles form the largest group of the reptile class and about 2,700 living species are known, classified in two large suborders.

The first suborder comprises the lizards (Sauria), which either have well-developed limbs, or (if the limbs are rudimentary or completely reduced) at least the remains of both the limb girdles and the sternum. Their movable ribs play an important role, as they permit the maximum flattening of their body, and the consequent exposure of a larger area to the rays of the sun, or greater contact with a warmed surface. The ribs are also used in gliding (Fig. 2). If limbs are present, they have variously formed digits, according to the environment of the animal. Good runners have long limbs with long, thin toes. The toes of the tropical lizards of the genus *Basiliscus* enable them to run over the surface of water or balance on aquatic plants. The scales on the toes of desert lizards of the genus *Eremias* are fringed to prevent the animals from sinking into the sand, while the undersides of geckos' toes are structured to allow these lizards to climb smooth vertical surfaces.

Tail adaptations are also of interest. Chameleons have a coiled, prehensile tail which fulfils the function of a fifth limb. The thick tails of some Australian geckos, skinks and spine-tailed lizard (*Uromastyx*) are actually fat deposits from which water is released during metabolism. The flying geckos of the genus *Ptychozoon* steer with their wide tail as they glide through the air. The spiny tails of girdle-tailed lizards (*Cordylus*) and the powerful muscular tails of monitors (Varanidae) are highly effective weapons.

The skull is movable, although less so than in snakes. The two halves of the lower jaw are fused in front, in the midline. Teeth are present along the edges of the jaws. Lizards have a remarkable faculty — the ability to cast off a part of their body (most often the tail) in the face of immediate danger. This property, known as autotomy, is most familiar in the true lizards (*Lacerta*), which willingly part with their tail when their life is at risk. They may even shed it in response to some internal stimulus, with no external interference at all. The tail does not snap between two vertebrae, but fractures across the weak centre part of a vertebra. The ends of the surrounding muscles and

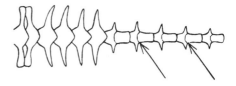

Fig. 4. At the base of a lizard's tail, fracture zones roughly in the middle of the body of some vertebrae can be seen. These are the site of autotomy, where part of the tail has been broken off.

skin overlapping the bony stump contract and close the wound. The broken part of the tail grows again (regenerates), but it is never as long as the original tail. The new scales also differ in appearance from the old ones, and are probably more primitive (Fig. 4). Geckos of the genus *Teratoscincus* are able to shed a part of their skin — sometimes over more than half of the total body surface. Before the skin regenerates, the geckos seek refuge in a damp situation, usually a rodent burrow.

The sense of sight is very well developed in lizards. The eyes usually have movable lids, but geckos and some skinks have fused lids like snakes, in which case the lids are transparent. A middle ear and an eardrum are present within a short auditory tube. Lizards are often characterized by marked secondary sexual dimorphism. Male true lizards (Lacerta) have a row of conspicuous femoral pores on the inner surface of their thighs, which exude a fatty secretion containing odoriferous substances known as pheromones. In addition, the males are usually more powerfully built and more brightly coloured (especially in the breeding season). They also have a more robust head than the females.

Lizards are mainly meat-eaters. Some species are oviparous, some ovoviviparous and others viviparous. They are divided into twenty families.

Snakes (Serpentes) comprise the other suborder. They have a characteristic long, limbless body and no longer possess a pectoral girdle and sternum, but there are a few (e.g. the Boidae) in which remains of the pelvic girdle have been preserved. Snakes have a remarkably lightly-built skull in which the freely movable, rod-like bones are joined together by ligaments. The two halves of the lower jaw are joined in the midline by an elastic, extensible ligament to enable the snake to swallow bulky prey. The teeth are long and sharp and are often connected to venom glands. The spine is composed of very many vertebrae (often as many as three hundred) with which the ribs articulate. The ribs are an important element in locomotion. Snakes have a particularly good sense of smell. They have a long, forked tongue which, when at rest, lies in a hard sheath on the floor of the mouth. It is both a tactile and an olfactory organ. In the auditory apparatus there is no middle ear or eardrum. The eyelids are fused and transparent and cover the eyes like a watch-glass. The outermost layer of the lids is shed along with the epidermis of the entire body. First the old epidermis on the edges of the jaws is loosened by persistently rubbing the head (and then the body) on rough objects. As soon as the epidermis has been detached, the snake, by further rubbing, turns it inside out and then crawls out of it. The epidermis is thus shed whole and not in fragments, as in lizards. In their new skins, snakes and lizards have a handsome gloss. Snakes have a dry and glandless skin, except for the scent glands in the anal region in some species.

The snake's alimentary system is adapted to the shape of its body and its habit of swallowing bulky food. The left lung is usually only rudimentary, while the right lobe is extremely long and part of it forms an air-sac. This comes into operation when the snake hisses and also acts as an air reservoir, so that even when the snake takes several hours to swallow its food it does not suffocate. In addition, the larynx lies well forward and during swallowing can be protruded in front of the chin, to facilitate the intake of air. Snakes, which are carnivorous, often take a very long time to digest their food. The large constrictor snakes (boas and pythons) can go without food for as much as a year. Secondary sexual dimorphism is frequent. For example, in boas, the rudiments of the pelvic limbs, which are outwardly manifested as claws on either side of the cloaca, are larger in the males than in the females. The sex of a viper can be told from its tail, the males having a long thin tail and the females a short, less tapering one. Most snakes are oviparous, but some species give birth to live young. Snakes are divided into eleven families containing a total of about 2,600 species.

Crocodiles (Order Crocodilia)

Crocodiles are the last order of reptiles. They are large animals with a long snout, an elongate body and a powerful tail and are adapted to an aquatic environment. They have powerful hind limbs and their body is covered with large bony plates and horny scutes. On either side of their head they have a pair of protrusible scent glands and further small glands are distributed over their body. Crocodiles exhibit a combination of very advanced characteristics (a heart with ventricles almost completely divided by a septum, differentiated dentition) and specialized characteristics (the ability to breathe with their nostrils showing above the water, while the mouth is open under the water, for example). They comprise tropical and subtropical species inhabiting sluggish rivers and lakes, while some species live in brackish water or in the salt water of an estuary. They are oviparous, the females laying their eggs in pits excavated in a river bank or on the shore. The females usually keep watch over the eggs and sometimes protect the newly-hatched young. Crocodiles actively hunt living prey in and beside the water, but they also eat animal refuse. Needless to say, they are excellent swimmers. They are divided into three families.

REPRODUCTION IN AMPHIBIANS AND REPTILES

Although people in general tend to place amphibians and reptiles in a single group, phylogenetically they are very far apart. The deep differences between the two classes are most apparent in their modes of reproduction.

Amphibians breed virtually in the same way as fishes, since the females deposit both eggs and larvae in water. There are, of course, many exceptions to this rule, especially where exotic amphibians are concerned. The eggs, which sometimes number several thousand, have a protein covering which swells up in the water. This provides protection for the embryos, ensures adequate moisture, concentrates the rays of the sun on the eggs (i.e. it functions like a lens), helps to anchor the eggs and is also the larva's first food. European amphibians mate after hibernation, when the males and females collect in a suitable body of water.

When European species of frogs and toads mate, the male usually sits on the back of the female and clasps her in a firm embrace. The female then slowly releases her eggs into the water, where they are fertilized by the male, seminal fluid of which is likewise released gradually. The eggs are thus fertilized outside the female's body.

Secondary sexual dimorphism is usually not very pronounced. The males are generally smaller, however, and in the breeding season they have prominent nuptial pads on their thumbs, to give them a firm grip on the female. Frogs and toads proclaim their territory vocally and their croaking is loudest at breeding time. The sounds are amplified by various resonance organs.

Tailless amphibians lay their eggs singly or in clusters. The organization of these clusters is often a characteristic feature and enables the eggs to be assigned to a species. The larvae (tadpoles) have little development at first. For several days they cling to the leaves of aquatic plants by means of special suction organs and, for the most part, remain motionless. Formation of the larval mouth is meanwhile completed and after this the tadpoles begin to eat. With their tiny horny teeth they scrape up algae or gather debris from the bottom of the pool. Tadpoles breathe by means of external gills which, unlike the gills of tailed amphibians (Urodela), soon become withdrawn into a branchial cavity behind the head. The respiratory cavities communicate with the surface by a single orifice (a spiracle) on the animal's side or abdomen. The covered gills atrophy and internal gills, with which the tadpole breathes until its metamorphosis, grow on the branchial arches. During their gradual metamorphosis the larvae acquire their forelimbs first. For a time these remain covered with skin, however, so that the first to be seen externally are the hind limbs. Later the forelimbs also appear and the tail shrinks. The gills gradually disappear and lungs develop. When metamorphosis has been completed the frogs (or toads) leave the water. The stump of a tail can still be seen on young frogs.

The way in which tailed amphibians reproduce is somewhat different. The males do not utter any sounds, but attract the females by means of intricate courtship displays which vary with the species. At this time sex-related differences between males and females are especially evident. The males are brightly coloured and develop conspicuous fin-like structures which aid identification between the two sexes. In most species of tailed amphibians the male germ cells are packed together in characteristic clusters enveloped in a gelatinous case. These are known as spermatophores. The male releases them and attaches them to leaves or sticks. The female picks them up with her cloaca and the eggs are fertilized inside her body. In some species (mainly those which occur in fast-flowing water), pseudocopulation takes place, with the male pushing the spermatophores directly into the cloaca of the female with his hind legs (e.g. the genus *Euproctus*). Tailed amphibians mate either in water or on land, but deposit the eggs (or larvae) in water. As with tailless species, the larvae are primitive and after a time undergo metamorphosis to the adult form. Unlike tailless amphibians, however, they retain external gills throughout the whole period of larval development. The larvae either have two pairs of limbs, or the forelimbs appear first. Neoteny is frequent among tailed amphibians, especially newts, and it is typical of the American Axolotl (*Ambystoma*). Apart from a few exceptions, European species do not look after their eggs or their young, indeed, cannibalism is more usual. Only a few tailed species give birth to fully-developed young. These develop in the widened ovaries of the female and are far fewer in number than the eggs of oviparous species. The reasons for this are obvious. The space available in which the young can develop is limited, and the survival rate is higher than in the case of eggs. Once laid, eggs are unprotected and losses are high among both eggs and larvae, so that only a few individuals reach adulthood.

As already mentioned, reptiles were the first completely terrestrial vertebrates. Their embryos therefore do not require an aquatic environment for their development, but develop on dry land. For this they need to be perfectly adapted. The eggs of reptiles, like those of birds and mammals, are protected from desiccation and damage by specific embryonal membranes (known as the amnion, chorion and allantois) and by a shell only partially permeable to water and gases. The embryo floats in the amniotic fluid, which gives it buoyancy and protects it from shock and from bumping or rubbing against the sides of the shell. Before the amniotic sac closes, a further embryonal membrane — the allantois — grows from the posterior part of the intestine of the embryo. The outer layer of the amniotic sac continues growing and again forms a double fold — the chorion or serosa — which encircles the entire amnion, the yolk sac and the allantois. The allantois and the serosa are responsible for the embryo's better nutrition, respiration and excretion.

Because of the immense evolutionary importance of the embryonal membranes, the higher vertebrate classes (reptiles, birds and mammals) have been placed together in a group termed Amniota (i.e. possessing an amniotic membrane), while the lower vertebrate classes (Elasmobranchii, i.e. fishes with a cartilaginous skeleton, bony fishes and amphibians) are included in the group Anamniota, as not possessing an amniotic membrane.

The way in which reptiles reproduce is incomparably more advanced than thàt of amphibians. The males have a protrusile copulatory organ — a penis — bearing fine barbs and a longitudinal groove. When at rest, the penis lies inside the cloaca. The penis is used to transfer the sperm cells during mating. The male introduces it into the cloaca of the female and fertilization thus takes place internally. The males of scaly reptiles (lizards and snakes) have paired organs or hemipenes, while chelonians and crocodiles have a non-paired penis.

Actual mating is usually preceded by a courtship ceremony or by duels between the males. The duels are generally intricate rituals, without bloodshed, ending in the retreat of the weaker party. Rival snakes, for instance, coil their bodies around each other and push and pull, but if they bite, venomous snakes do not discharge their poison. Male lizards are generally brightly coloured during the breeding season. Reptiles mark out their territory in different ways — geckos acoustically (i.e. with their voices), some lizards optically (i.e. with their brightly coloured throats, by poses and by movements) and snakes and other lizards olfactorily (or chemically, i.e. by scent). The latter apply secretions from their femoral pores to raised features in their territory and to their beaten paths, deposit faeces or smear these places with the everted wall of their cloaca. Being long-lasting, such markers are very effective.

Most reptiles are oviparous. The eggs are wrapped in a parchment-like envelope (snakes and lizards), or have a hard, chalky shell (geckos, crocodiles and chelonians). When first laid the eggs are pliant, since the shell takes several hours to harden. The eggs of geckos are also sticky and can be made fast behind bark and in crevices. When laying their eggs, female geckos use their hind legs to aid the process. The size and weight of eggs without a chalky shell increase during embryonal development due to water uptake. The female lays her eggs in clutches in one or in a number of holes dug in a suitably moist, sun-warmed substrate. The right temperature and moisture content are the most important factors in the incubation of the eggs. The young hatch fully-developed and differ from their parents only in size and sometimes in colouring.

The females of some species of lizards and snakes do not lay eggs, but give birth to fully-developed young. The embryos undergo their entire development in the body of the female and are born the instant when, or just before, they leave the egg and the membranes. Embryos which develop inside the female have neither a tough nor a chalky shell, but are wrapped in fine membranes. Sometimes (as in vipers) the female may give birth to several young and then lay eggs as well. Ovoviviparity is commonest among reptiles living in cool regions, such as the Viviparous Lizard, the Adder and the Slow-worm. True viviparity, when the embryos receive their nutrition from a uterine secretion or a primitive placenta, is known in only a few species of Australian skinks.

Most reptiles do not brood, or guard their eggs, although some females (e.g. among geckos and cobras) remain near them. Pythons (Pythoninae) give their eggs the most care, since the female not only protects them, but also keeps them warm. By wrapping herself round the eggs, she can raise the temperature in the centre of the coils by as much as 12 °C compared with the temperature outside, so that the body forms a kind of natural incubator. Female crocodiles watch over their eggs, and in some species they actually help the newly-hatched young to find their way out of the nest. Before hatching, the young make sounds, to which the female responds by scratching away the pile of earth covering the eggs. For a few days afterwards, the female guards her young.

CIRCADIAN AND SEASONAL RHYTHMS

The rhythm of amphibian activity in the course of a day is closely correlated to changes in their environment. The limiting factor for terrestrial species is moisture, which appears in large amounts on the surface of the soil and vegetation during the night, so most amphibians are nocturnal animals. Amphibians living in water, however, often hunt during the daytime and at night.

Reptilian circadian activity is primarily dependent on the environmental temperature. Every species has its optimum temperature, which varies from 20 to 40 °C. Most reptiles like warmth and consequently, in the temperate belt, species active during the day preponderate, while the number of species active in the evening is smaller and the number active at night smaller still. In environments where the ground becomes exceedingly hot during the day, as in desert and open steppes, reptiles prefer to come out after dusk or at night, when the ground cools to a bearable temperature.

Circadian rhythms also alter during the year. For example, in the spring the Adder comes out of hiding at midday, when the sun is at its hottest. Later in the year it emerges twice a day — once in the early morning and again after dusk. Members of the same species behave differently in the northern and southern parts of their area at the same time of year and differently at low and high altitudes. The temperature dependence of reptiles is thus a prime factor in the cyclic character of their life.

The seasonal rhythm of the life of amphibians and reptiles is very complex. Their blood temperature is not constant, but depends on, and varies with, the temperature of their immediate environment. Such animals are described as ectothermic. Birds and mammals keep their body temperature constant by means of thermoregulation and are thus endothermic.

In the temperate latitudes, where temperature conditions vary markedly during the year, amphibians and reptiles are also obliged to adapt their yearly rhythms to the vagaries of the climate. In winter, therefore, they hibernate. In the autumn they look for a place which will give them shelter, and where they will not freeze to death. Such places are generally few and far between and it is thus by no means uncommon to find a large number of individuals, often belonging to different species, hibernating together. For example, deep rubble slopes in forests, loose stone walls and terraces and deserted mine adits are patronized by fire salamanders and toads. Similarly, groups of snakes, often of different species, appear near deep rock fissures before the onset of winter and again in the spring. Snakes congregate near their winter quarters several weeks before they actually start to hibernate. During the warmest part of the day they bask in the sun, but show no interest in food. Gradually, as the temperature falls, they penetrate deeper and deeper into the security of their subterranean shelters and finally stay there.

Physiological functions are reduced to a minimum during the period of full hibernation. When spring and warmer weather come round again, the temperature of their environment rises, and so, in consequence, does that of the hibernating reptiles and amphibians. The animals then begin to emerge, first of all for just a short time during the warmest part of the day and again without eating. After this transition period, as the environmental temperature steadily rises, they disperse. Some species mate before leaving their winter quarters, since collective hibernation simplifies the problem of finding a partner. Others move in large numbers to the nearest source of suitable water in order to mate, and are to be seen at this time on roads cutting across their route.

Amphibians and reptiles sometime aestivate. This is the reverse of hibernation, for the animals 'sleep' during the summer. Physiologically, apart from the higher body temperature, there is no difference between the two. The animals seek shelter during the height of summer, when high environmental temperatures are combined with lack of water. Aestivation gives important protection against desiccation and overheating.

COLOUR ILLUSTRATIONS

Fire Salamander
Salamandra salamandra Salamandridae

The Fire Salamander, which attains a length of about 20 cm, is one of the largest and most handsomely coloured amphibians in Europe. Large numbers of ducts from cutaneous glands open on to its smooth body. The glands produce a poisonous secretion which, together with the animal's gaudy yellow-black colouring, protects the salamander from its foes. The short-toed limbs are adapted to a terrestrial mode of life.

A nocturnal animal, the Fire Salamander comes out of hiding during the daytime only after heavy rain. With its sluggish, awkward movements it is able to catch only the slowest prey, such as snails, slugs, certain beetles, myriapods and various types of worms.

The Fire Salamander inhabits deciduous woodland, especially beechwoods, over the greater part of Europe and in north-west Africa. The adult animals are not themselves restricted to areas where there is water, but they need it for reproduction. The female gives birth to the larvae by night, depositing them in the clean, cool water of forest streams and springs. A few South European populations living in dry regions are an exception. Here the females give birth to fully metamorphosed young and have no need of water for reproduction. Salamanders mate on dry ground. The male attaches his cloaca to that of the female and then releases his semen. The sperm cells survive for a long period in the female's body and the larvae are usually not born until May or June of the following year. The larvae, which can number up to 70, are about 3 cm long and have two fully-developed pairs of limbs. They live and develop in the water for 2 to 3 months before undergoing metamorphosis and leaving the water, although sometimes they hibernate and metamorphosis does not take place until the following spring. Salamanders reach sexual maturity in their fourth year. They are solitary, but often hibernate in groups. Hibernation begins in November, when the salamanders hide away in rubble, caves and rocky terraces.

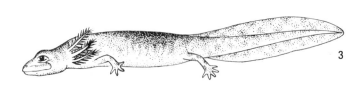

3

Owing to its vast area of distribution, the Fire Salamander has about 15 geographical forms or subspecies. The typical form, *Salamandra salamandra salamandra* (1), lives in eastern Europe. The most striking in appearance is the west European subspecies, *S. s. terrestris*. Its spots merge to produce continuous bands running the length of its body, with yellow as the dominant colour (2).

The cutaneous gland ducts can be seen clearly behind the eyes, as dark dots in the large, kidney-shaped parotoid glands. Although its feet are not webbed, the salamander is a good swimmer. By pressing its limbs to its sides and undulating its body in the same way as a snake, it can move very quickly. Even the youngest larval stages possess all their limbs, a caudal fin-like structure bordering the tail, and large branched external gills (3).

29

Alpine Salamander
Salamandra atra
Salamandridae

This salamander measures not more than 16 cm in length and is thus smaller than the preceding species. It abounds in parts of the Alps and in the mountains of Yugoslavia south of Albania. Generally it is to be found at altitudes of 700—2,800 metres. There have been several reports of findings of the Alpine Salamander in the mountains of central Europe, but they always proved to be a case of mistaken identity. The animals were usually found to be the dry land phase of the Crested Newt or an atypical black aberration of the Fire Salamander.

The unicoloured, glossy black body of the Alpine Salamander has pronounced ribbed segments, which give it the appearance of a quaint plastic toy. It inhabits mountain forests and when preparing to hibernate can be found in vast numbers in its hibernation area.

It has the same type of diet as the Fire Salamander and it also feeds on slow-moving arthropods, worms and molluscs, which it hunts mainly at night. It emerges in the daytime after heavy rain, especially if the rain follows a period of drought. Otherwise it hides away during the daytime, under stones of fallen tree trunks, or in rock fissures which hold moisture. Since it mainly inhabits limestone mountains where flowing water is in short supply, it has evolved a special form of care of its young. The female is fertilized on dry land, as in the case of the Fire Salamander, but pregnancy lasts for two years or even longer, and she gives birth — again on dry land — to fully-developed young.

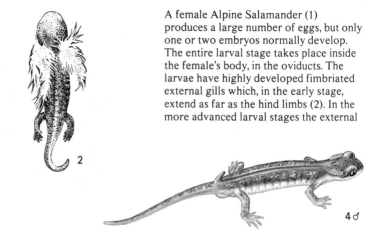

2

A female Alpine Salamander (1) produces a large number of eggs, but only one or two embryos normally develop. The entire larval stage takes place inside the female's body, in the oviducts. The larvae have highly developed fimbriated external gills which, in the early stage, extend as far as the hind limbs (2). In the more advanced larval stages the external

4 ♂

1 ♀

3

gills gradually disappear. The young (3) are deposited directly on the ground, in a damp spot under stones.

Asian members of the Salamandridae are mostly brown. One of them, Luschan's Salamander, *Mertensiella luschani,* which occurs mainly in Turkey, is also to be found on some of the islands in the Aegean. The male has a curious soft, curved projection above the root of its tail (4).

31

Spectacled Salamander
Salamandrina terdigitata   Salamandridae

This handsome salamander occurs in Italy, but is missing throughout a zone running down the Adriatic coast. It has a predilection for hilly country and is seldom to be found at high altitudes, the maximum height at which it has been reported being 1,300 metres.

It is a small animal, measuring roughly 10 cm together with its tail, and is the only European salamander with four toes on every foot. Unlike the majority of tailed amphibians, its limbs are not capable of regeneration. Its tail is almost cylindrical, has a sharp ridge both above and below and accounts for three-fifths of the total length of the animal.

This salamander inhabits damp, shady spots near streams and drying ponds, to which the females come to lay their eggs early in the spring. Neither the males nor the females remain long in the water and later they are more likely to be found under stones or among fallen leaves. They come out of hiding after dusk to hunt for the small insects (especially ants) and spiders which constitute their diet. They are seldom to be seen in the hottest summer months and experts suppose that they aestivate (spend the summer in a state of torpor, the converse of hibernate). On the other hand, they can often be seen during the winter months and it is therefore assumed that they do not hibernate.

Another small species is the slim brownish-black and yellow-spotted salamander, the Caucasus Salamander *(Mertensiella caucasica)* which inhabits the banks of mountain torrents in the Caucasus. Because of its nimble movements it resembles a lizard rather than a salamander.

3

32

Between its prominent eyes the
Spectacled Salamander has light
markings which resemble spectacles and
on its body jt has distinct segments
formed by folds of skin (1). The bright
red underside of its tail has a warning
function (2). When in danger, the
salamander curves its tail over its back
and the bright colour of the tail,
contrasting sharply with the plain,
dark-coloured back, keeps many
a potential enemy at a safe distance.

   The Golden-striped Salamander,
Chioglossa lusitanica (3) is
a golden-yellow, slim-bodied salamander
inhabiting Portugal and a small adjoining
part of Spain. As in the case of
Mertensiella its nimble movements give it
a close resemblance to a lizard. It is
active after dusk. For one third of its
length its tail is cylindrical and then it
gradually flattens out. In adults the tail is
usually double the length of the body.

1

2

Sharp-ribbed Salamander
Pleurodeles waltl

Salamandridae

The Sharp-ribbed Salamander is the largest European amphibian. Occasionally it attains a length of 30 cm, but mostly it only reaches about 20 cm. It occurs in the greater part of the Iberian Peninsula and in Morocco. Another species, *Pleurodeles poireti,* also lives in northern Africa.

This salamander has no dorsal crest, but in both sexes the tail is bordered by a caudal fin. The granular epidermis contains a large number of cutaneous glands.

The Sharp-ribbed salamander inhabits slow-flowing water, water-filled ditches, lakes, marshes and reservoirs. During the daytime it hides in a tangle of aquatic plants and swims out in search of food after dusk. It is a good swimmer and leaves the water only if the source dries up. In this event these animals are to be found on dry land, especially under stones, where the soil retains at least some of its moisture.

The salamanders breed twice a year. — early in spring and at the height of summer. Each year the female lays up to 1,000 eggs, which she attaches, in short chains, to aquatic plants. The larvae have an apparently insatiable appetite and consequently grow very quickly.

This is a popular aquarium animal and under favourable conditions it can survive in captivity for up to twenty years. It is also important in the laboratory where it is used in physiology experiments. Feeding presents no difficulties, as its staple diet is wireworms and earthworms and it will also eat small pieces of lean meat.

The most characteristic feature of the Sharp-ribbed Salamander is the bright orange tubercles on its sides, in which the sharp ends of its ribs can be felt (1).

The Tiger Salamander, *Ambystoma tigrinum* (2), which measures up to 30 cm and lives in lowland areas of Mexico and the United States, can develop in an unusual way. If the water contains

3

sufficient iodine, in a few weeks the larva turns into a fully-developed terrestrial salamander, while if it does not, the large larva persists in a neotenic form, i. e. it retains its larval form, but is capable of reproduction. Another species, *Siredon mexicanum,* which is better known as the Axolotl, is kept in the neotenic form by many fanciers and also by research laboratories. In addition to normally coloured individuals, albino mutants of the Axolotl are often encountered (3). If larvae of both the above species are given thyroid extract (which contains iodine) or actual thyroid, they metamorphose into adult animals and live on dry land.

1

Pyrenean Brook Salamander
Euproctus asper
Salamandridae

The members of the genus *Euproctus* occur chiefly in mountainous regions and are seldom found in the lowlands. The altitude of their localities is in the range 250—3,000 metres, but these salamanders are to be found most frequently at 700—2,500 metres. All three species frequent similar habitats. During the daytime these salamanders hide away under stones or fallen tree trunks beside mountain streams and lakes, or retire to damp gullies where the temperature does not exceed 15 °C and the ground does not dry up. In some localities they have also been found in caves. At night they emerge to hunt for food — small invertebrates, especially worms and gastropods. They hibernate below ground in winter, and may also aestivate in summer.

The Pyrenean Brook Salamander breeds at the end of spring and beginning of summer in clear, cold water. The eggs are 5 mm in diameter and are attached to submerged stones. The animals mate by pseudocopulation. The male twines his tail round the female, thereby ensuring close contact of their cloacae, and uses his hind legs to thrust the spermatophores (capsules containing the sperm cells) directly into the female's cloaca. This avoids unnecessary loss of sperm in the flowing water. The eggs take about four weeks to develop in the cold water and it is a year before the young salamanders leave it.

Males can be distinguished from females by their rounder cloaca, the spur-like outgrowths on their hind limbs and their more strikingly coloured throat.

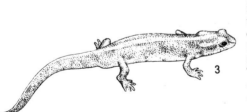

Salamanders of the genus *Euproctus* inhabit small, non-overlapping areas in the Mediterranean region (2). The largest of them is the Pyrenean Brook Salamander, *Euproctus asper,* which can measure as much as 16 cm in length (1). The nominate subspecies *Euproctus asper asper* lives in the Pyrenees, while *E. a. castelmouliensis* has been found near

Bagnères-de-Bigorre in France. (The nominate subspecies carries the same name as the species and is the form from which the species itself was described.)

The Sardinian Brook Salamander *(E. platycephalus)*, which measures up to 14 cm (3), lives only on Sardinia and the last member of the species, the Corsican Brook Salamander *(E. montanus)*, which

1

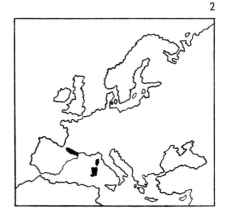

2

is somewhat smaller, has been found only on Corsica. All the species have a thick, conspicuously granular skin and small or completely vestigial parotoid glands.

The Painted Salamander, *Ensatina eschscholtzi* (4), which measures 7 — 15 cm and inhabits North America, has a similar mode of life to that of the members of the genus *Euproctus*. It is one of the three species comprising this genus and occurs only in mountainous regions.

Marbled Newt
Triturus marmoratus
Salamandridae

In France, where the western border of the distribution area of the Crested Newt ends, the incidence of the Marbled Newt — one of the handsomest tailed amphibians in Europe — begins. Its area comprises the whole of the Iberian Peninsula as well as south-western France. The interrelationship of the two species is demonstrated by the frequent crosses often described by scientists in the past as separate species. It was not until investigations were carried out on captive newts that classification of these two large species of newts was satisfactorily achieved.

The Marbled Newt attains a maximum length of 14 cm. Its green ground colour is broken by black marbling, while its abdomen is grey. Black dots — the ducts of cutaneous glands — are clearly discernible in the green patches. Both sexes during the terrestrial phase of their life, and the females during the aquatic phase also, have a bright orange or red stripe running down the middle of the back right to the tip of the tail.

This species has less dependence upon water than the Crested Newt. It frequents springs, streams and pools, usually in woods, only during the short breeding season and spends the greater part of the year on dry ground. At this time, its skin is dry and rough to the touch. Like all European newts, if it loses a limb, or even a more complex organ, such as a jaw or an eye, it is able to grow a new one.

Because of its attractive appearance the Marbled Newt is often kept in terraria and it reproduces normally in captivity.

2 ♂

3

The annual life cycle of the Marbled Newt (1) is similar to that of other European members of the genus *Triturus*. As soon as the warm spring weather wakes them from their winter sleep, the newts make for the water. Their skin is at first rough and dry and the secondary sexual characteristics of the males are not accentuated, but once in the water the males acquire a conspicuously cross-striped dorsal crest terminating above the base of the tail. Along the sides, roughly in the middle, the tail has a silvery stripe and it is bordered by an enlarged fin-like structure (2).

Some newts leave the water soon after mating, while others remain in the water for a considerable time. As a rule, the females stay there longer than the males.

The genus *Triturus* is not represented on the American continent, where it is replaced by similar genera, such as *Diemictylus* and *Taricha*. Fig. 3 shows the Californian Newt, *Taricha torosa*.

1

Alpine Newt
Triturus alpestris Salamandridae

The Alpine Newt inhabits a relatively large area in the middle of Europe. In the west it extends into France, an isolated population is known in the north-west of Spain and it also inhabits northern Italy and part of the Balkan Peninsula. Its characteristic colouring makes confusion with other species impossible. It has a special predilection for forest pools in hilly country, and in mountainous country it ascends to an altitude of 2,500 m. Occasionally it can be found in deep pools formed by forest streams or, at low altitudes, in ponds among fields and meadows.

In central Europe it occurs at moderate altitudes, most frequently in the cold water of flooded stone quarries in the middle of woods. Here the first newts appear at the end of March and remain in the water until July or August. After leaving the water the males lose their crest and the skin of both males and females acquires a finely warty appearance. The newts then live on dry land until the autumn, when they look for a suitable place to hibernate. They spend the winter in the soil, in rotting tree stumps or under stones.

The females are usually larger than the males, with a total length of 12 cm. If picked up, the Alpine Newt inflates itself and lets the air out with a whistling sound.

This newt is capable of complete regeneration of digits or of whole limbs. Sometimes individuals can be found having five digits — a phenomenon known as polydactylism.

Some ten subspecies of the Alpine Newt have so far been described, but in some cases the distinction appears to have been unwarranted.

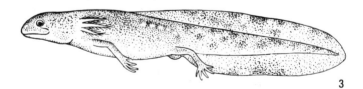

3

The sex of an Alpine Newt can be established relatively reliably. The female is less colourful and often has marbled markings (2), while the male has bright blue sides and a low crest (1). The eggs are laid singly on submerged plants. The larvae, which hatch in 15—20 days, have gills and clearly discernible rudimentary forelimbs. The hind limbs appear during later development. Strikingly large dendritic gills and a wide fin-like structure bordering the tail are

characteristic of the maturing larva (3).
In cold water with a poor supply of
nutrients, it often happens that the larvae
do not complete their development by
the autumn. In this case they hibernate
and metamorphosis takes place the
following year. In rarer cases neoteny has
been recorded, i. e. the fully-grown larvae
do not change to the terrestrial form, but
are nevertheless capable of reproduction.

2 ♀

1 ♂

Crested Newt, Warty Newt
Triturus cristatus   Salamandridae

The Crested Newt is the largest of the European newts. It measures 16 cm and occasionally up to 18 cm in length. Its ground colour and markings, the colouring of its abdomen and the shape of the male crest are very variable. Four subspecies are known. The Northern Crested Newt, *(Triturus cristatus cristatus),* is found in England and Scotland, from the middle of France to the Urals and from southern Scandinavia to the Alps. The Alpine Crested Newt, *(T.c. carnifex),* lives in Austria, northern Yugoslavia and Italy. The Danube Crested Newt, *T. c. dobrogicus,* inhabits the Danube basin (in Czechoslovakia, intermediate forms between this and the nominate subspecies are known). The last subspecies, the Southern Crested Newt, *T. c. karelinii,* occurs in the eastern part of the Balkans, the Crimea, Asia Minor and northern Iran.

The Crested Newt usually lives, together with the Smooth Newt, at low altitude in various types of still or slow-flowing water. It also occurs, in suitable water, at fairly high altitudes. It remains longer in the water than any other European newt and can stay there almost permanently. Its food comprises aquatic insects, their larvae and various worms, and it can also extract aquatic gastropods from their shells. Large specimens are highly predacious and attack the larvae of other amphibians and other newts, including members of their own species. A fully-grown crested newt is able to swallow an adult smooth newt. In the terrestrial phase of its life, the Crested Newt is active only at night or during damp weather. It hibernates on dry ground. In captivity it has been known to live for as long as 20 years.

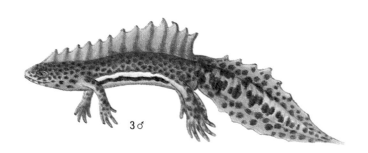

3 ♂

During the aquatic phase of its life, the Crested Newt displays very marked secondary sexual dimorphism. The males have striking crests (1). The dorsal crest is high and dentated and is distinctly separate from the caudal crest. The females (2) have no dorsal crest and only a narrow border on the tail.

Another large newt, the Banded Newt, *Triturus vittatus* (3), which attains a length of up to 14 cm and is one of the most colourful species, lives in the Caucasus, Asia Minor and Syria. It inhabits mountainous regions at altitudes of 1,000 — 1,600 metres (in rare cases up to 2,800 m), where it frequents cool, shady spots beside mountain streams with rocky bottoms. In the summer, when the streams dry up, it hides under stones and rotting tree trunks and is hard to find.

Smooth Newt
Triturus vulgaris
Salamandridae

The Smooth Newt is one of the most abundant European amphibians. It is distributed over the whole of Europe, including Great Britain and Ireland, and in the temperate belt it extends as far as the Altai Mountains. In Europe it is absent only on the Iberian Peninsula and in the south of France and Italy. It forms about ten subspecies over its entire distribution area, but the question of its taxonomy is still unresolved and some subspecies seem to be merely local colour variants.

It primarily colonizes the margins of stretches of standing water or the banks of slow-flowing rivers in low-lying country. Occasionally — mainly in the southern parts of its area — it is to be found in the mountains, at altitudes up to 1,500 metres. It is very common in cultivated country, but is now endangered there by the increasing use of chemicals in agriculture and forestry.

The Smooth Newt feeds on various invertebrates — aquatic or terrestrial, according to the time of year. The aquatic phase of its life lasts from April to June, when breeding takes place. They then leave the water and secrete themselves in damp, shady spots under stones, in rotting wood or in moss. They also hibernate in such surroundings, often in large groups.

It is not uncommon to find single specimens or whole populations of the Smooth Newt which never leave the water. These undergo neoteny and, while retaining some of the characteristics of the larval stage, including its appearance, are able to reproduce without completing metamorphosis.

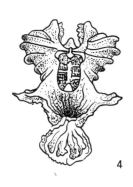
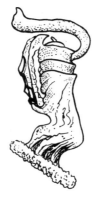

4

The Smooth Newt is characterized by very marked sexual dimorphism, especially in the aquatic phase of its life, and the sexes are easily distinguishable at first glance. The male (1), which is the larger and may measure up to 10 cm, is more brightly coloured and has a continuous crest stretching from its head to the tip of its tail. In the smaller female (2), only the tail has a narrow border.

In newts, mating is accompanied by complicated courtship displays (3) characteristic of every species, in which the males move backwards and forwards, vibrating their tails. They turn to the female head first and lay their tail against

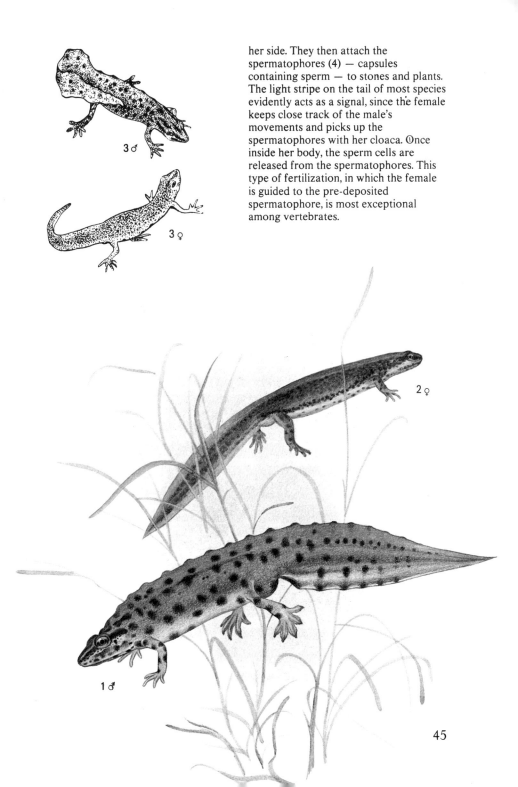

her side. They then attach the spermatophores (4) — capsules containing sperm — to stones and plants. The light stripe on the tail of most species evidently acts as a signal, since the female keeps close track of the male's movements and picks up the spermatophores with her cloaca. Once inside her body, the sperm cells are released from the spermatophores. This type of fertilization, in which the female is guided to the pre-deposited spermatophore, is most exceptional among vertebrates.

3 ♂

3 ♀

2 ♀

1 ♂

45

Montandon's Newt
Triturus montandoni
Salamandridae

During the aquatic phase of its life, the colouring of the adult Montandon's Newt is very variable and the size and number of its spots also vary. Its general appearance, however, is not conspicuous, and both sexes resemble the female Smooth Newt. Even in the breeding season the males are not more strikingly coloured or adorned, apart from having a slightly wider border on the tail. The filamentous process at the end of the male's tail, the unicoloured abdomen and the prominent ridges down the back give this newt a strong resemblance to the Palmate Newt, *Triturus helveticus,* of western Europe. Furthermore, comparison of the areas of distribution of the two species leads to the conclusion that the species evolved together until their original large area of distribution was broken up (evidently during the ice ages), when the eastern population developed separately and a new species was formed. Isolated findings of Montandon's Newt in Germany in the first half of the present century support this theory. A detailed study of the relationships between the two species could produce interesting results.

Male specimens of Montandon's Newt attain a maximum length of 7 cm, while the females reach 10 cm. They chiefly inhabit warm still water over a muddy bottom, but also occur in pools of spring water at altitudes up to 2,000 metres. Their stay in the water is comparatively short and as soon as mating is over and the eggs have been laid they leave it for dry land. During the daytime they hide under stones or rotting tree trunks in deciduous woods and conifer forests. Their diet consists of a variety of invertebrate animals found in the humus layer. Sometimes the larvae also hibernate and do not undergo metamorphosis until the following year.

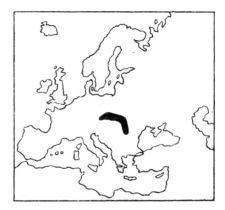

3

The distribution area of Montandon's Newt is very small and comprises the Carpathian mountain system, minus the most easterly part (3). In Czechoslovakia this newt has also been found in the Jesenik highlands in northern Moravia. The males do not have a dorsal crest during the breeding season, but only a fin-like border on the tail. The terminal filament on the tail of the male measures up to 8 mm (1), but the female has no such filament (2). One of the most characteristic features of this species is that the body is very square in cross-section, the cause being the prominent ridges which run down the animal's back (4). The skin is rough, especially during the terrestrial phase of the newt's life, when it is a plain rusty brown colour all over. Several cases of hybrids between Montandon's Newt and the Smooth Newt have been known. These animals had a longer terminal filament and only a narrow dorsal crest.

4

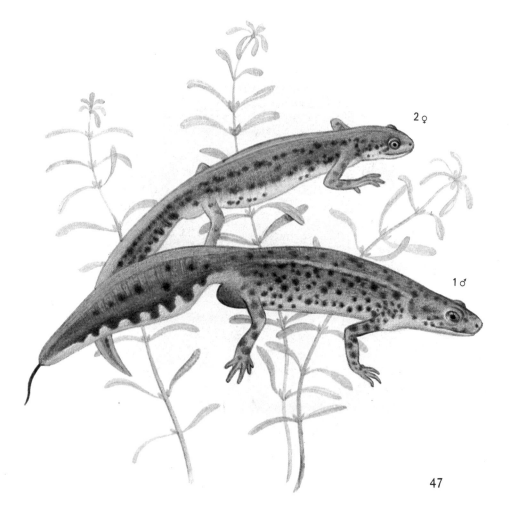

2 ♀

1 ♂

Palmate Newt
Triturus helveticus   Salamandridae

As already mentioned, this species is in many respects morphologically similar to Montandon's Newt, but has an entirely different distribution area which nowhere overlaps that of the other species. It inhabits a large part of western Europe, to the north-west of the Iberian Peninsula in the south, and to Great Britain, including Scotland, in the north. Its adaptability to different altitudes is considerable and interesting. In coastal regions it colonizes ponds and marshes with brackish water, while in northern Spain, in the Pyrenees, it ascends to altitudes up to 2,000 metres.

Both sexes have ridges along their sides, giving the body a square appearance. The abdomen is generally plain yellow, or only slightly spotted, and the throat is pink. The males are characterized by a filamentous process about 5 mm long at the tip of the tail. They do not possess a pronounced dorsal crest, but only a fin-like border to the tail. At first glance the female is hard to distinguish from the male, but her caudal fin is narrower, it has no filamentous process and the spots on her body are smaller.

The Palmate Newt breeds in different kinds of still water, including brackish water. The female lays her eggs in March and after four months of larval development in the water, the fully metamorphosed young, measuring 3 cm, emerge on to dry land.

The Palmate Newt has a similar life cycle and diet to Montandon's Newt.

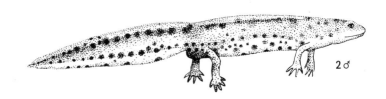

2 ♂

Unlike the male Montandon's Newt, the hind feet of the Palmate Newt (1) are webbed.

Bosca's Newt, *Triturus boscai,* (2) is a species inhabiting the western half of the Iberian Peninsula. It closely resembles the preceding species, but the males never have a filament at the tip of the tail, which merely tapers off to a sharp point. This newt lives mainly in small ponds, but has also been found in lakes inside caves.

The Italian Newt, *Triturus italicus*, from southern Italy, is the smallest of the European newts. Its maximum length is 7.5 cm, but it usually measures only 5—6 cm. The male has no dorsal crest and only an insignificant border on its tail.

All newts shed their skin from time to time. They peel it away from their jaws by means of their legs and then, with their legs and mouth, strip it off in one piece, right to the tip of the tail (3). Quite often they eat the old skin.

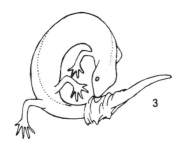

3

1 ♂

49

Italian Cave Salamander
Hydromantes italicus

The family Plethodontidae, with approximately 175 species, is distributed mainly over America and has only two representatives in Europe. One feature they all have in common is that they are all lungless. Respiration takes place over the whole of their epidermis and their highly vascularized oral mucous membrane. They have an anatomical peculiarity in the form of an almost immobile lower jaw and when swallowing prey this salamander moves only its upper jaw.

The Italian Cave Salamander measures just over 10 cm. It has a wide head and large, prominent eyes, and it hunts its prey by sight. It inhabits the mountainous regions of northern and central Italy and the south of France. At lower altitudes it can be found at the foot of mountains, especially where there are underground labyrinths or rock fissures into which rainwater trickles. It frequents only moist, shady places with a relatively low temperature, and does not tolerate high environmental temperatures.

It can climb nimbly over vertical rock faces, helped partly by a sticky substance secreted by its epidermis and partly by its prehensile tail. To catch the small arthropods and molluscs which form its staple diet it also climbs plants.

Little is known of its reproduction, but it is presumed that the female gives birth to fully-developed young. Among specimens kept in captivity, young measuring about 3.5 cm appeared in the terrarium and immediately — and very actively — began catching small insects.

The members of the genus *Hydromantes* are characterized by their limbs, which have five toes and interdigital webbing (2). The webbed feet come in useful for climbing the perpendicular walls of caves rather than for swimming, however.

The Italian Cave Salamander (1) has evolved a curious way of catching its prey. It approaches to within 3—5 cm of an unsuspecting insect, and then suddenly, like a lightning, shoots out its long, rod-like tongue, which terminates in a flattened adhesive disc (3). Before the insect knows what is happening, it vanishes into the salamander's mouth and is eaten.

The other European member of the family is the Sardinian Cave Salamander, *Hydromantes genei,* which inhabits the mountains of Sardinia (4).

Olm, Cave Salamander
Proteus anguinus   Proteidae

This most curious of European tailed amphibians did not become known to science until 1875, when it was discovered in the Postojna Cave in Yugoslavia. Today some fifty caves in the limestone mountains along the Adriatic coast of Yugoslavia and one isolated spot in Italy are known to be inhabited by olms.

The water in underground caves is practically devoid of vertebrates and this makes the Olm a striking phenomenon there. After heavy rain, olms may be washed out of their subterranean haunts into open streams, where they tend to collect in deep pools. The Olm is characterized by a white, unpigmented skin, which completely covers its eyes, and by three pairs of external gills which it retains all its life. Olms also have lungs and the breathing of atmospheric oxygen is evidently more important for them than branchial respiration. Experiments have confirmed that olms literally drown if they have no opportunity of surfacing for air.

Olms feed mainly on water fleas and other aquatic crustaceans. These they are able to track down by means of sensory organs in their skin, since their skin-covered eyes are able to perceive only light and shadow. They do not leave the water voluntarily and have seldom been found away from it. The subterranean water in which they live has a temperature of 5—10 °C. The female usually gives birth to two larvae about 1 cm long, but if the water is warmer she may lay up to 80 eggs. Little is known of the way in which the larvae develop, or how long their development takes.

2

The Olm (1) generally measures 25—30 cm. Its puny limbs are out of all proportion to the length of its body. The forelimbs have three and the hind limbs two stunted digits.

Other species of the family Proteidae occur in America. The best known is the Mud Puppy, *Necturus maculosus,* an inhabitant of the eastern part of North America, which lives in open water and not underground. The Texas Blind Salamander, *Typhlomolge rathbuni* (2), first found in a well near San Marcos in Texas, is adapted to a subterranean mode of life. It belongs to the family Plethodontidae and has a most grotesque appearance.

1

Yellow-bellied Toad
Bombina variegata Discoglossidae

In small puddles on forest footpaths on hills and mountains what seems to be an inconspicuous little toad — the Yellow-bellied Toad — can be encountered. If it is caught and turned over, however, the colouring of its underside, including the limbs, is found to be almost tropically exotic. The purpose of this brilliance is to keep enemies at bay. If the toad is attacked it turns over on to its back, forming either a concave or convex arch and displaying its 'war paint'. Its defences also include a venomous secretion, produced by cutaneous glands, which stings when it comes into contact with mucous membrane. If children rub their eyes after handling this toad they usually require medical attention.

The Yellow-bellied Toad inhabits the whole of central and western Europe except the Iberian Peninsula, and in the east it extends beyond the Carpathian Mountains. It is a typical aquatic toad and is to be found in small village ponds, even those highly contaminated by natural organic substances, as well as in forest pools and in puddles. It measures approximately 5 cm.

From May to July the female lays over 100 eggs and the larvae (tadpoles), which are about 6 mm long, hatch twelve days later. The tadpoles from late eggs do not undergo metamorphosis in the same year, but hibernate in the larval state. The adult toads hibernate in the ground.

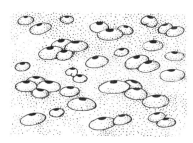

2

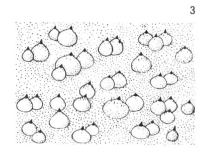

3

The nominate species, *Bombina variegata variegata* (1), occurs in central Europe, *B. v. kolombatovici* in Dalmatia, *B. v. pachypus* in Italy and *B. v. scabra* in the southern part of the Balkan Peninsula. Sometimes specimens with an orange or bright red abdomen, resembling the related Fire-bellied Toad, may be found. In the Yellow-bellied Toad, however, the light pigmentation of the abdomen accounts for over 50 per cent of its body area, whereas in the Fire-bellied Toad the light area is smaller than the dark. The shape of the warts on the skin is an important differential character. Those of the Fire-bellied Toad have a blunt, tough tip (2), while the skin of the Yellow-bellied Toad is covered with small, sharp, horny spines and is rough to the touch (3).

Fire-bellied Toad
Bombina bombina Discoglossidae

The distribution area of the Fire-bellied Toad stretches from the Volga basin to Denmark. Unlike the preceding species it occurs at low altitudes. It inhabits different types of still water, from tiny pools in swamps to village ponds and large lakes. Throughout the summer, but mainly in May, June and July, when the toads breed, the dolorous nasal croaking of the males can be heard. If large numbers of them sing in chorus, the sound is like a distant rumbling, and it comes as a surprise to find that the source of such a loud noise is small toads less than 5 cm long.

Like the Yellow-bellied Toad, the Fire-bellied Toad is diurnal. It chiefly frequents vegetation either beside or floating on the water, where it can conceal itself. It is a good diver and is easily able to catch the small aquatic arthropods on which it chiefly feeds. It consumes all the stages in the life cycle of the mosquito, and is thus of importance in the control of this insect pest. On their throat the males have a subcutaneous vocal sac, which is noticeable only when it is inflated (male yellow-bellied toads have no such sac). When the toads emit their call, the vibration creates rings in the water around them, and although they can also make the sound under water, there it is not so loud.

The Fire-bellied Toad does not form any subspecies. Where its area of distribution overlaps that of the Yellow-bellied Toad hybrids are occasionally found. If their source of water dries up, these toads convert to a terrestrial mode of life. They hide away in fissures in the dry, cracked mud and hunt terrestrial prey, such as small beetles and two-winged insects.

The skin of the Fire-bellied Toad similarly secretes an active toxin which produces a burning sensation when it comes into contact with human mucous membrane.

2

3

The Fire-bellied Toad (1) has darker spots on its back than the Yellow-bellied Toad. Part of its back is sometimes bright green, making it hard to distinguish among patches of algae floating on the water, and although the orange or vermilion colour of its abdomen is very conspicuous, its area is smaller than the darky pigmented part (2). In captivity the Fire-bellied Toad has been known to live to the ripe old age of 30 years.

The handsome Oriental Fire-bellied Toad, *Bombina orientalis* (3), has abdominal markings which are finer and form bizarre curves. It is imported from the Far East and kept in terraria. In the wild it lives in bamboo groves in the mountains but knowledge of its biology is very meagre. The largest representative of the family is the Chinese *B. maxima*, which measures up to 8 cm. In this species, even the tadpoles have a fiery red abdomen. All discoglossids lay their eggs on aquatic plants, singly or in small groups (4).

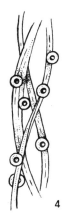

4

1

Painted Frog
Discoglossus pictus   Discoglossidae

Like the whole of the family, this little frog takes its name from its disc-shaped tongue. This, except for a small part of its margin, is fixed, so that it cannot be protruded and its owner has to catch prey with its jaws. The frog feeds on a variety of aquatic and terrestrial invertebrate animals and on small fishes which it occasionally catches in shallow water.

The Painted Frog inhabits the south of France, the Iberian Peninsula, Sicily, Malta and northern Africa from Algeria to Morocco. It grows to a length of over 7 cm and is highly dependent upon water. It is even to be found in brackish water, so salty that other amphibians shun it. It inhabits marshes, ponds and flowing water in low-lying country, is very agile and hunts both during the daytime and by night.

Since they breed often and easily, discoglossids are popular model animals in laboratories, where they are used chiefly for embryological studies. Under natural conditions the female lays 300—1,000 minute eggs over a period of 2—10 days, on a stony substrate. Here they are fertilized by the male. Both the eggs and the tadpoles develop very quickly and metamorphosis is completed within one or two months, according to the climatic conditions. Eggs are laid several times a year, again depending on the climate, so that discoglossids appear in large numbers in their own localities.

The Painted Frog is very appositely named. In general it resembles frogs of the genus *Rana,* both in shape and colour and also as regards its biology. Like a true frog, it has long hind legs and a smooth skin. Its colouring is very variable. It usually has different kinds of spots, those on the back being arranged in three main rows (1). In one of the more frequent types there is a pronounced light stripe down the middle of the back (2), as in the Marsh Frog, for instance.

The Tyrrhenian Painted Frog, *Discoglossus sardus* (3), which differs only slightly from *D. pictus* (chiefly by its wider head) and is regarded by some experts as merely a subspecies of the latter, has been found on the islands of Corsica, Sardinia, Giglio and Monte Cristo and on the Îles d'Hyères.

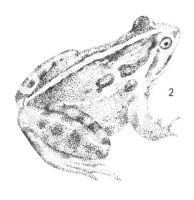

2

1

Midwife Toad
Alytes obstetricans Discoglossidae

This inconspicuous little toad, which measures barely 5 cm, is indeed very appropriately named, on account of its most unusual and extremely interesting breeding habits. Between April and August, each female is courted by a number of males, until the strongest of them finally succeeds in embracing her. Then he encourages her, with movements of his hind legs, to lay her eggs. To make the situation even more unique, this process does not take place in water, as is usual with frogs, but on dry land. As the female releases the eggs, the male fertilizes them and winds the whole string of 50—80 large eggs round its own hind legs. The female's task is then over and the rest of the care of the eggs falls on the male's shoulders (or rather on his legs). The male carries the eggs about with him wherever he goes, sees that they have the correct amount of moisture and do not dry up, shelters with them in a hole in the ground during the daytime, and first thing in the morning moistens them with dew or dips them in shallow water. After about a month he makes for suitable still water, and here the tadpoles hatch. It is about a year before the tadpoles undergo metamorphosis and are able to leave the water.

The Midwife Toad has a similar mode of life to that of the true toads. During the daytime it hides under stones or in holes which it excavates in the ground. Its diet consists of a variety of invertebrate animals. It can be distinguished immediately from a true toad by its vertical pupils. The male Midwife Toad has an agreeable, sonorous call.

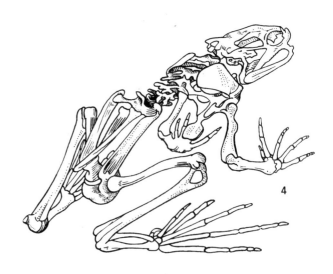

4

The Midwife Toad (Fig. 1 shows the male) inhabits western Europe from France to the Harz Mountains and western Thuringia in Germany. The related Iberian Midwife Toad, *Alytes cisternasii,* inhabits the western and middle part of the Iberian Peninsula. The main difference between the two species is the number of tubercles on the palm of the hand, the Midwife Toad having three (Fig. 2), the Iberian Midwife Toad having only two (Fig. 3).

Except for a few bones, frogs have a completely ossified skeleton (4). The number of vertebrae varies from 7 to 9 and in individual species three types of vertebrae are found, the shape of which is the main criterion for the division of frogs into suborders. The ribs of frogs are generally poorly developed and do not therefore participate in respiration, their role being taken over mainly by the muscles used for swallowing. The forelimbs are shorter than the hind limbs and have four digits, while the hind limbs have five. The skull is primitive.

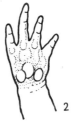

2

3

1 ♂

Common Spadefoot
Pelobates fuscus Pelobatidae

The Common Spadefoot is a robust toad which gives an impression of being clumsy, although the reverse is actually the case. On dry land it proceeds with quick leaps and in the water it dives just as skilfully as an aquatic toad. Characteristic of the genus is the slit-like, vertical pupil, which can be dilated, however, showing that the toad is a nocturnal animal. Only a few good students of nature have actually encountered this toad, although it is commoner than is normally supposed.

Dykes, loose forest soil and even tilled fields and gardens are favoured by the Common Spadefoot. The best place and time to catch these frogs is the vicinity of shallow ponds in low-lying country at night, with a torch. As soon as it starts to get light, the toads bury themselves quickly and skilfully in the ground to a depth of 1 metre by means of a sharp outgrowth on their hind limbs. They dig backwards, their rear end disappearing first and their head last. In the daytime they come out only after heavy rain. After a heavy downpour in an acacia grove in central Hungary, the ground literally opened and hundreds of spadefoots swarmed out.

The Common Spadefoot is 8 cm long, but its tadpoles — the largest in Europe — can measure 18 cm. When picked up the toad utters squeaking sounds and its skin glands release a secretion which smells like garlic. It feeds on insects, worms and molluscs. It has a large area of distribution stretching from Siberia to France. It does not occur on the Iberian Peninsula.

2   3

The Common Spadefoot is to be found in water from April to June, but it leaves as soon as the eggs have been laid. The eggs are laid in wide gelatinous bands (4), each female laying up to several thousand eggs. During the breeding season these toads give forth guttural sounds.

The distribution area of the Western Spadefoot, *Pelobates cultripes*, (2) lies roughly to the west of the area of the Common Spadefoot (1) and stretches from western France over the whole of the Iberian Peninsula. This toad measures 10 cm. Intermediate to these two species in size is the Eastern Spadefoot, *P. syriacus* (3), which occurs in the Balkan Peninsula and western Asia.

All species of spadefoots are very variably coloured and their chief differential characters are their size and the shape of the metatarsal protuberance or 'spade' on their hind limbs. The metatarsal tubercle on the hind foot of the Common Spadefoot is illustrated in Fig. 5.

Parsley Frog
Pelodytes punctatus   Pelobatidae

This inconspicuous, robust little frog measuring about 5 cm cannot be correctly classified as a member of the Pelobatidae without an examination of its eyes, which have a vertical pupil. Otherwise, at first glance, it looks more like a small Common Frog.

It inhabits the Iberian Peninsula, France, western Belgium and a small part of north-western Italy. Everywhere it occurs in extremely damp habitats or directly beside water, but it makes its presence known only after rain or at night, when it emerges from its hiding places under stones or in holes in the ground. The chances of finding it are better in spring, when the frogs, which are very good swimmers, enter the water to breed. The males can be heard from below the surface. The females lay 1,000–1,600 eggs in jelly-like strings on aquatic plants. Although the frogs are small, the tadpoles measure up to 6.5 cm.

The other species of the genus *Pelodytes, P. caucasicus,* is found far away in the mountains of the Caucasus, where it occurs at altitudes of up to 2,300 metres. Like the Parsley Frog, it leads a very secluded existence and feeds on various invertebrate animals which it catches during the night. Unlike *P. punctatus* it lays its eggs in clusters of 160–500. The tadpoles are 5 cm long and metamorphosis takes place after about 80 days.

These frogs have been observed in water near Lake Rica in the Great Caucasus at the end of August. Larvae resulting from mating so late in the season do not undergo metamorphosis during the same year, but hibernate in the larval state on the bottom.

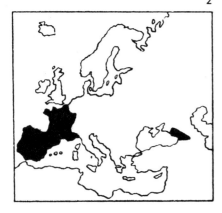

2

Neither *Pelodytes punctatus* (1) nor its only relative, *P. caucasicus,* forms any subspecies.

The marked discontinuity in the area of distribution of the genus *Pelodytes* is very interesting (2). In the past these evolutionally ancient frogs were evidently far more numerous, but only two species have survived to the present day.

Their developmental cycle is in general uniform. In a few days the small, and at first incompletely developed, larvae (4) hatch from the fertilized eggs (3). The time between laying and hatching varies, depending on the species and the temperature of the water. The tadpoles breathe by means of gills — first external, then internal — and they have a special suction organ enabling them to cling to aquatic plants or to stones. First to grow are the forelimbs, but they remain below the skin, so that the first to be seen are the hind limbs (5) and the forelimbs appear later (6). The tail then disappears (7), sacculate lungs develop, the gills degenerate and (in most species) the fully-developed frog leaves the water.

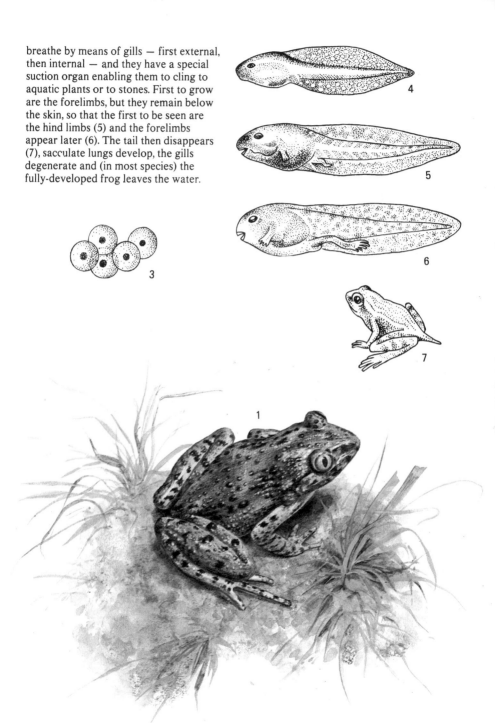

65

Common Toad
Bufo bufo
Bufonidae

During its terrestrial phase the Common Toad is variably coloured, from yellowish to greyish-brown and almost black. In the water, however, it is mostly light yellowish-brown. It is a nocturnal animal and can be seen during the daytime only when there is a heavy rain, or in the breeding season. The females measure up to 15 cm, but the males are distinctly smaller.

Early in the spring (in central Europe generally at the end of March), hundreds of these toads travel long distances to their breeding site, which is usually a pond in a wood or field. If the water covers a large area they remain in a narrow zone round the edge. In the breeding season the males utter muffled sounds audible only over a short distance, since they do not possess an external resonator to amplify their voice. Nevertheless, the sounds are strong enough to tell the females where they can find a partner. For the rest of the year the toads are silent. The difference in the size of the sexes is most obvious at the time of mating, when the tiny male perches on the back of the bulky female and holds her in a tight embrace.

The female lays up to 6,000 eggs in strings over 2 metres long. Development from egg to fully developed toad takes 2–3 months. The tadpoles form shoals and feed on algae.

The vast distribution area of the Common Toad includes practically the whole of Europe, including Great Britain, and the temperate zone of Asia, including Japan.

The Common Toad is in great danger of extinction at the hands of man — probably more than any other of its kind. Thousands of these animals die under the wheels of cars during the spring trek to their breeding sites and many others are killed through prejudice or ignorance.

5

The Common Toad (1) is man's most valuable ally in the biological fight against field and garden pests. Being nocturnal, it fills in the time when insectivorous birds are asleep, and it also devours various larvae and gastropods which come out only at night.

These toads hibernate in the ground. Except during the mating season they are solitary, having their own places of refuge, which they excavate themselves, and their own hunting grounds. With their highly-developed sense of local orientation, they always return 'home' safely after hunting or laying their eggs. They feed on arthropods, molluscs and worms and the larger females also catch frogs and mice.

The three European species of the genus *Bufo* can be distinguished by the soles of their hind feet: Common Toad (2), Green Toad (3), Natterjack (4).

Toads have cutaneous glands which secrete active toxins. These deter many predators, but they do not harm the Grass Snake. When the toad encounters such a snake it swells up and stands on its hind legs, so that it looks double its normal size. Sometimes this form of defence is actually effective (5).

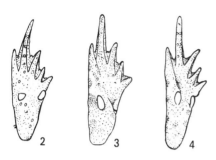

2 3 4

1

Natterjack
Bufo calamita
Bufonidae

A small toad which runs instead of leaping will almost certainly prove to be the Natterjack. The reason for this unwonted form of locomotion is that the toad's hind legs are shorter than usual, being roughly the same length as its fore legs. The Natterjack attains a maximum length of 8 cm, but generally measures only 5 cm. It can be distinguished from the Common Toad by its bright green irises (the irises of the Common Toad are amber).

The Natterjack frequents countryside comprising large stretches of unfertile soil on a sand or clay base. Its relatively large area of distribution is made up of the whole of the Iberian Peninsula and the greater part of western Europe, and stretches across Czechoslovakia and Poland to the Baltic countries. However, its populations are small, the toad is not active until after dusk, its colouring is inconspicuous and it is only a small animal, so not surprisingly it is generally overlooked.

Below the throat the males have a barely discernible vocal sac. In the mating season they summon females from far away with a relatively loud croak which sounds rather like a ratchet.

The female lays 3,000–4,000 eggs in single or double strings, usually late in the spring or in early summer. It deposits them in small, transitory pools which later dry up, with the result that the larvae develop quickly. Near the sea the larvae also develop in brackish water.

The Natterjack has a similar diet and similar habits to other species of true toads.

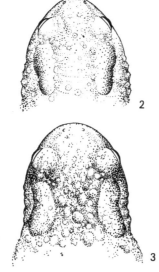

2

3

In addition to the lenght of its limbs and the colour of its irises, the Natterjack (1) can be identified by the yellow stripe which runs right down the middle of its back. The largest glands on the body of a toad are the paired parotoid glands on the upper part of its head behind its eyes, which secrete large amounts of a frothy substance containing an active toxin. The shape of the glands is a characteristic of each species and in the case of European species can be used for their differentiation. In the Common Toad they are crescent-shaped, with out-curved tips (3), while in the Natterjack and the Green Toad they are straight (2).

1

4 ♀

The tropical and temperate belts of the Earth are inhabited by about 500 species of true toads. A few species, often brightly coloured, live in North America. One is *Bufo canorus*, which occurs in the mountains of the Sierra Nevada. The black markings on the female are in sharp contrast to the light green ground colour (4).

Green Toad
Bufo viridis

Bufonidae

The Green Toad can be seen on warm nights, in places where one would never expect to find amphibians at all. It can survive through long droughts and at high temperatures, in hide-outs which it often excavates itself. It may equally well be encountered on the seashore, on dry steppes and in damp localities. Quite often it occurs near human dwelling places, the toads assembling in the evenings and at night to catch insects attracted by the street lights. Insects are the main component of its diet.

Its area of distribution comprises the whole of Europe except the British Isles, the Iberian Peninsula and part of France, and it extends to Mongolia in Asia and to northern Africa. In the mountains of Asia it has been found up to 4,500 metres, but in central Europe it generrally avoids high altitudes. The nominate form lives in Europe, while Africa and Arabia are inhabited by the subspecies *Bufo viridis arabicus.* Hybrids of the Green Toad and the Natterjack have been found on several occasions.

Female green toads, which measure about 10 cm, are both larger and plumper than the slim males, which are further distinguished by a well-developed vocal sac below the throat. The males produce sounds during the breeding season, their very agreeable, tinkling calls, which sound more like the trilling of a canary, being uttered while they squat in the water. Isolated males remain in the water and can still be heard in June.

The Green Toad has a slimmer body and longer limbs than the Common Toad, and is consequently both nimbler and faster.

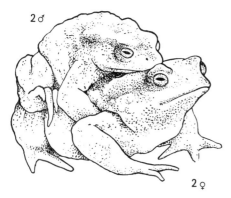

2 ♂

2 ♀

The Green Toad (1) is the prettiest and most strikingly coloured of all the European true toads, with circumscribed greyish-yellow spots and bright red tubercles standing out sharply against a light background. Green toads have clearly discernible eardrums.

These toads breed in April and May. They are not particular about the quality of the water and will even make do with a polluted village pond or with part of a sewer. During mating, while the male grips the female with his forelimbs (2), the female lays up to 12,000 eggs in gelatinous wrappings 2—4 metres long.

70

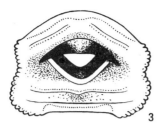

3

4

The tadpoles, which hatch in 4—5 days, take two to three months to develop. Before their metamorphosis is completed they measure 4.5 cm and are thus the largest tadpoles of any of the European true toads.

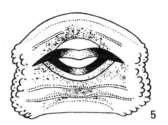

5

The main difference between the tadpoles of European toads is in the shape of the mouth, as well as in their size: the Green Toad (3), the Common Toad (4) and the Natterjack (5). In shallow water the tadpoles sometimes dig depressions at regular intervals and spend a considerable amount of time in them, picking algae and debris from the bottom.

1

Common Treefrog
Hyla arborea
Hylidae

However much some people object to frogs, they nevertheless regard the dainty little Common Treefrog with favour, partly because of its neat appearance and its pretty colouring, but also because of the superstition which still prevails, that its croaking foretells a change in the weather. Experience has refuted this belief and it is now known that the frogs also call when the sun is shinig and are silent on cold, wet days.

The Common Treefrog is distributed over a vast area stretching from north-western Africa across the whole of Eurasia (except the British Isles) to the Japanese archipelago. Its northern limits roughly coincide with the distribution of geographic forms (subspecies), five of which occur in Europe alone.

This terrestrial frog measures up to 5 cm. The smoky grey or yellowish-brown throat of the male is darker than that of the female. Adult treefrogs usually spend all their time on trees and bushes or in tall grass, whereas young ones are to be found mainly on the ground. The frogs are also encountered at considerable distances from water, except in the mating season. The loud, guttural call of the males can be heard the whole year round, but they are especially noisy in the breeding season. Treefrogs feed mainly on insects collected from plants, although large specimens may also catch small vertebrates. When swallowing their prey they use their forefeet to help them.

One of the most important characteristic of treefrogs is their ability to change colour. Time depends chiefly on the temperature of the environment and the mood of the animal. The normal protective grass green colour can change to grey, brown or a yellowish colour, or spots may even appear.

The area of the nominate subspecies *Hyla arborea arborea* (1) extends from the north of Spain and from northern and central France to the Caucasus and the Ural Mountains.

3

2 ♂

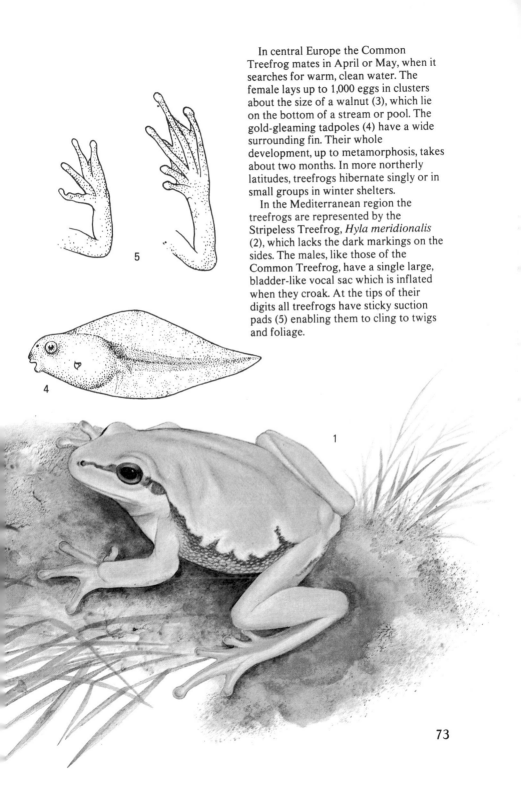

In central Europe the Common Treefrog mates in April or May, when it searches for warm, clean water. The female lays up to 1,000 eggs in clusters about the size of a walnut (3), which lie on the bottom of a stream or pool. The gold-gleaming tadpoles (4) have a wide surrounding fin. Their whole development, up to metamorphosis, takes about two months. In more northerly latitudes, treefrogs hibernate singly or in small groups in winter shelters.

In the Mediterranean region the treefrogs are represented by the Stripeless Treefrog, *Hyla meridionalis* (2), which lacks the dark markings on the sides. The males, like those of the Common Treefrog, have a single large, bladder-like vocal sac which is inflated when they croak. At the tips of their digits all treefrogs have sticky suction pads (5) enabling them to cling to twigs and foliage.

Common Frog
Rana temporaria

Ranidae

The Common Frog inhabits the whole of northern and central Europe and in Asia it occurs as far as Japan. In addition to the nominate subspecies there are two other subspecies in Europe, *Rana temporaria honnorati,* which lives at the foot of the Alps, and *R. t. parvipalmata* of north-western Spain. The Common Frog is not restricted to a specific type of habitat, but is to be encountered in both still and running water, in damp woods and marshy meadows and often far away from water. It also ascends high into the mountains and has actually been found at an altitude of 4,000 metres. It catches various invertebrates — snails, worms, beetles, hymenopterous insects and other arthropods.

The frogs usually hibernate in water (in the mud on the bottom), but immature individuals often hibernate on land, in sheltered damp areas under stones or fallen tree trunks. In the spring they are the first frogs to re-emerge.

Adult common frogs may measure up to 10 cm, but are usually smaller, particularly the males. The males can also be distinguished from the females by the blue colouring of their vocal sac during the breeding season and by the conspicuous dark nuptial pads on their thumbs, which always swell in the mating season. Since the males have internal, paired resonance organs, barely discernible from the outside, their call is indistinct. They are to be heard during daylight, but hold no nocturnal concerts. They croak only when in the water and never on dry land.

There are gourmets who claim that the legs of the Common Frog taste better than the legs of other species. The frogs are not seriously threatened, however, since they live singly and catching them is very laborious. The fact that they are not totally dependent upon water also means that they do not suffer if there is a shortage of suitable, unpolluted habitats and they therefore remain the most abundant frogs of central Europe.

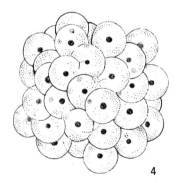

4

The Common Frog is extremely variable in colour with a brown or russet back and a light-coloured and frequently diversely spotted underside. The characteristic dark facial 'mask' extends to its forelimbs (2). Green species of *Rana* in Europe have no 'mask' (3). The Common Frog (1) has a wide, rounded and relatively short head with a blunt-tipped snout. It also usually has a heavily spotted abdomen. The spot on its temples is sometimes rather indistinct.

2

3

The breeding season begins in March, when the nights are still frosty and the frogs are surrounded by loose ice. The females lay up to 4,000 eggs in clusters (4) which float in the water like lumps of jelly. The newly-hatched tadpoles cling to the leaves of aquatic plants (5). Their development takes 2—3 months. When their metamorphosis has been completed, the young frogs leave the water in large numbers.

5

1

Moor Frog
Rana arvalis
Ranidae

The Moor Frog is the rarest member of the brown frogs of central Europe, but its large area of distribution extends from France, across central Europe, to Lake Baikal in Russia. In the north, in Sweden, it occurs beyond the Arctic Circle. The places where it is most likely to be found are peat bogs or damp meadows in areas where ponds abound. Its incidence is now generally confined to a few scattered populations, since the number of suitable meadows has markedly dwindled in the past years. A decrease in this species has also been recorded in a number of localities where meadows never treated with chemicals were used for keeping domestic geese. In two years the frogs had vanished, hounded to death by the greedy geese.

In early spring, when the nights are still frosty, small groups of moor frogs assemble in pools and small ponds. If the pond is large, they form an isolated society in just one part of the shallowest water. In the mating season the males acquire a bluish or deep colouring, especially on the throat, as a result of the infiltration of lymph into subcutaneous spaces.

On dry land the Moor Frog has a curious form of defence against its enemies. First it executes a long, high jump. This is followed by a series of quick scrabbling movements as it burrows at the foot of a clump of grass. This method often saves it from storks and other predators.

It hibernates at the bottom of a pool or on dry land, and has a diet similar to other frogs.

4

It is not easy to distinguish the Moor Frog (1) from the related Common Frog, but if they can be observed side by side, they can be more easily differentiated. For one thing, they have differently shaped heads, the Moor Frog having a more pointed snout. There are also

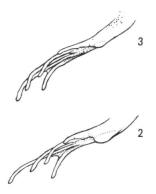

differences in the shape and size of the metatarsal tubercle on the medial aspect of the soles of the hind feet. The Moor Frog has a large hard tubercle two-thirds the size of the first digit (2), while the Common Frog has a small, soft protuberance (3). The Moor Frog's abdomen is light and unicoloured, although occasionally there may be small spots on the throat and chest. The dark spots on the temples are very distinct.

Several species of the genus *Rana* also occur in North America. One of the most popular is the Leopard Frog, *Rana pipiens* (4), which is used as a laboratory animal.

Agile Frog
Rana dalmatina

Ranidae

The area of distribution of the Agile Frog stretches from the north of Spain, across France, central and southern Europe and Turkey to the Caucasus and the Ural Mountains. This frog likes warmth and does not therefore have an even distribution. It inhabits only very warm and particularly low-lying places. It can be encountered most frequently in damp, shady spots on the fringes of deciduous or mixed woods and in riverside meadows. The only time it actually enters water is in the breeding season. The poorly developed webbing between its toes also marks it as a terrestrial animal.

Like other members of the family Ranidae, it occasionally eats small vertebrates as well as invertebrates (mainly spiders).

In central Europe the Agile Frog mates in March or April, but in the more southerly parts of its area the breeding season begins in February. The female lays 600—1,000 eggs, mainly at night, depositing them in clusters. The tadpole is a light olive brown in colour. Prior to metamorphosis it may measure as much as 6 cm and is thus one of the largest European tadpoles. In central Europe metamorphosis takes place from June to August, and when it is over the young frog leaves the water.

The males can only be heard during the breeding season. They do not possess a vocal sac and their voice is hardly more than a barely audible croak. There are no fundamental outward signs of sexual dimorphism, but the males usually hibernate in still water, on the pool bottom, and the females in hiding places on the land.

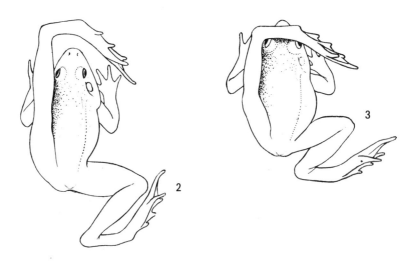

The Agile Frog (1) is a brown frog. It forms no subspecies. It is very similar in colour to the two preceding species, but has fewer spots. Behind each eye it has a dark temporal spot. Its snout is flat and pointed and its eardrums are very close to its eyes. In central Europe it seldom attains a length in excess of 6 cm, but further south it may measure up to 12 cm.

The most striking feature of this species is the extremely long, slim hind legs. If they are stretched forward along the body, the heels reach beyond the tip of the head (2), while in other European brown frogs, such as the Common Frog (3), they are never more than level with the tip of the head.

Its long limbs and slim body enable this frog to jump long distances. Leaps 2 m long and 0.75 m high have actually been measured.

1

Stream Frog
Rana graeca

Ranidae

This frog inhabits the middle and southern part of the Balkan Peninsula and Italy and it probably occurs occasionally in southern parts of Switzerland.

It is to be found chiefly in mountain areas and it usually lives in coniferous forests or in mixed woodland, near forest streams. It is seldom encountered at low altitudes. It is one of the smaller true frogs measuring no more than 7.5 cm in length. It forms no subspecies and it is therefore interesting to note that specimens collected in Italy have a shorter body and shorter limbs than individuals from the Balkan Peninsula.

The Stream Frog is closely related to the Common Frog and, like its relative, can tolerate a wide temperature range. It is active from early spring until late autumn, when the first night frosts drive it into hiding. A sudden change to warmer weather brings it out again, however. It hibernates buried deep in loose forest soil, beneath fallen leaves, in tree stumps, under boulders or in any kind of hole in the ground. It takes to the water for only a short time in spring, when breeding takes place. The female lays clusters of eggs in quiet backwaters where the flow of the stream is not too strong, or in small forest lakes. For the rest of the year the frogs live singly, like most other members of this family. Their diet consists mainly of insects and insect larvae, various kinds of land worms and slugs.

The colouring of the Stream Frog (1), as well as its biology, is similar to that of the Common Frog. It can be distinguished by the dark spot on its throat.

The Iberian Frog, *Rana iberica* (2), inhabits Portugal, north-western Spain and Andorra. This inconspicuous animal, which measures about 5 cm, also lives mainly in mountain forests, where it occurs at altitudes of more than 2,000 metres.

2

1

Further species of brown frogs live in the forests of the Caucasus. One of them, the Long-legged Wood Frog, *R. macrocnemis,* attains a length of over 8 cm, but biologically it is no different from the rest.

Some brown frogs can be differentiated by the markings on the throat: *R. graeca* (3), *R. iberica* (4), *R. dalmatina* (5) and the Italian Agile Frog, *R. latastei,* (6).

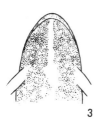

3

4

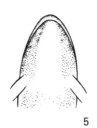

5

6

Marsh Frog
Rana ridibunda

Ranidae

Today the tendency of the Marsh Frog to spread slowly westwards and replace the original species, the Edible Frog, not only as a competitor for food, but as an actual predator, can be witnessed.

The Marsh Frog inhabits a large area extending from northern Africa across southern and central Europe to western Asia. The nominate subspecies occupies the greater part of this area. Two others are less widely distributed and in places the different areas overlap. *Rana ridibunda perezi* lives mainly on the Iberian Peninsula and in north-west Africa, while *R. r. saharica* occurs from Algeria, across Egypt, as far as the Caucasus.

The Marsh Frog is the largest of the original European frogs. Normally it measures 10—12 cm, but some specimens measuring up to 17 cm have been found. The males are smaller than the females. The size of these frogs is determined by the variety of their diet, which, apart from insects, includes small vertebrates, such as frogs, lizards and voles, and tadpoles caught in shallow water. Marsh frogs mainly inhabit warm lowlands where there is an adequate supply of shallow ponds or where there are large, slow-flowing rivers. Quite often they form large communities with as many as 2,000 animals per hectare.

The frogs hibernate in the mud at the bottom of a pool and do not reappear until the temperature of the water rises to 6—9 °C. When the water temperature reaches 15 °C the females lay their eggs in large clusters which remain at the bottom of the pool. The number of eggs depends on the size of the female. For example, a 9-cm female lays about 4,000 eggs, a 10-cm female some 5,000 and an especially large female up to 12,000. The light green tadpoles have a pear-shaped body and can grow to a length of 9 cm, but the newly metamorphosed frogs measure only 1.5—2.5 cm. Metamorphosis takes place after three months' development in the water.

2 ♂

The Marsh Frog (1) is very variably coloured and the markings on its back are also highly individual. Its ground colour is generally olive green, but sometimes it is mainly brown. The eardrums of the male are always grey or blackish-brown.

In similar habitats in central and eastern Europe can be found the smaller related Pool Frog, *Rana lessonae* (2), the systematic classification of which is still under debate. A subspecies, *R. l. pannonica*, has been described in Yugoslavia.

3

4

5

The three species of green frogs found in Europe can be distinguished by the length of their hind limbs: *R. ridibunda* (3), *R. esculenta* (4) and *R. lessonae* (5). Positive identification, especially of young animals, is made difficult by variability within each species and by the existence of various intermediate forms and possible hybrids.

1 ♂

Edible Frog
Rana esculenta
Ranidae

The Edible Frog is the best-known species in the group of green frogs — a group which gives systematists and taxonomists a headache, since it causes them great difficulties in classification and presents many unexplained problems.

The Edible Frog inhabits the whole of Europe except the Iberian Peninsula and the northern part of Scandinavia. In the east it extends to the Volga. It never occurs at altitudes above 1,000 metres, but otherwise it is very common and has no particular environmental requirements. Its incidence is highest in regions containing large numbers of shallow ponds, but it also inhabits small isolated lakes and pools. Edible frogs are famous for their concerts, rendered on warm nights. Their food is sought both in water and on land and is very varied. They consume all kinds of insects and other invertebrates and also attack small vertebrates, including their own species. In some localities the Edible Frog is being progressively pushed back by the larger Marsh Frog.

In spring the females lay their eggs in the space of one or two days. Individual clusters contain not more than 300 eggs, but the total number laid by one female is 5,000—10,000. The development of the larvae, which hatch in 10 days, depends on the temperature. In warm weather it takes about three months, but sometimes the larvae hibernate and do not undergo metamorphosis until the following year.

The reason this frog is called *esculenta* (= edible) is that it is the main source of the popular 'frog's legs'.

The Edible Frog (1) is a moderately large member of the family. Sexual dimorphism is manifested primarily in size, the females measuring 9 cm and the males not more than 7.5 cm, though very occasionally specimens measuring up to 12 cm may be encountered. At the corners of the mouth the males have a slit, through which, when they croak, their whitish or grey vocal sac swells out like a balloon. Edible frogs have prominent, striking and often differently coloured ridges along their back and down the centre of their back they frequently have a yellowish green stripe.

The American Bull-frog, *Rana catesbeiana*, (2) originated in North America, but it was taken to some of the Caribbean islands and then introduced in Europe, where it is now found chiefly in northern Italy. It resembles European frogs and its diet also includes small vertebrates. Its powerful voice sounds more like the bellowing of a bull than the croaking of a frog.

Hermann's Tortoise
Testudo hermanni   Testudinidae

Land tortoises are the most familiar, but also the most endangered of the reptiles. Over a long period, huge numbers of them have been caught and exported to countries further north — partly as pets (when they usually suffer an early death) and partly as a culinary delicacy. The outcome has been a severe reduction in their numbers in their natural surroundings and for some species the situation has become so catastrophic that they are no longer encountered at all in places popular with tourists.

Two subspecies of Hermann's Tortoise inhabit southern Europe. *Testudo hermanni hermanni* occurs in southern Italy, the Balkans and south-eastern Rumania, while *T. h. robertmertensi* lives in the south of France, eastern Spain and central Italy and on Corsica and Sardinia. Both of them attain a length of about 25 cm. (The given length refers to the direct distance between the anterior and posterior margins of the shell, i. e. not over the top of the carapace.)

This tortoise is mainly herbivorous, feeding on leaves, tender shoots, grass and fallen fruit, but given the opportunity it also eats offal, faeces and slow-moving invertebrates.

It inhabits dry localities in low-lying country and often lives directly on the seashore. In the more northerly parts of its area of distribution hibernation lasts from October to March, but further south it is of shorter duration. The hard-shelled eggs, which are white and round, have an average diameter of 40 mm and weigh 10 g. The female lays them between April and June, and buries them in the ground. They number 2—5, according to the size of the female. The young tortoises hatch in 8—12 weeks and measure about 4 cm. Incubation time depends on the temperature round the eggs.

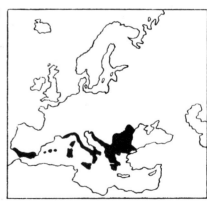

Hermann's Tortoise (1) and the Spur-thighed Tortoise, *Testudo graeca,* (2) are very similar. The latter inhabits southern Europe, north Africa and south-western Asia and forms four subspecies. Both the above tortoises are similarly coloured, have the same biology and are often mistaken for one another. It is not very difficult to distinguish between them, however. The Spur-thighed Tortoise usually has a single, undivided supracaudal plate, while in Hermann's Tortoise the supracaudal plate is divided into two (4). The tail of Hermann's Tortoise terminates in a horny plate and it has a group of large scales on the upper part of its hind limbs near the tail (4), whereas the Spur-thighed Tortoise, in the same position, has small scales and among them, on either side, a single prominent scale projecting like a spur (3). The possibility of reciprocal crosses between the two species sometimes hampers correct determination. In both, the limbs are adapted to life on dry land. The neck can be withdrawn S-wise inside the shell. This property is shared by the members of the families Testudinidae, Emydidae, Chelydridae and a number of other families not named in this book.

The map (5) illustrates the distribution of European members of the genus *Testudo.*

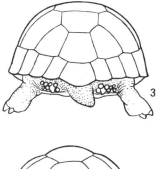

3

4

1

Marginated Tortoise
Testudo marginata

The Marginated Tortoise is the largest land tortoise in Europe. It grows to a length of up to 35 cm and older specimens may weigh as much as 6 kg. Its incidence is confined to a relatively small area in south-eastern Greece, from Mount Olympus to the Taiyetos Mountains. It has recently been found several times on Sardinia, but no doubt found its way there through the agency of man. No subspecies have been found, but *T. marginata* — *T. graeca ibera* hybrids born in captivity are more characteristic of the Marginated Tortoise.

The Marginated Tortoise lives on dry, sunny scrub-covered hillsides, but remains close to water. It is active during the day, especially in the morning and early evening. In the heat of noonday it prefers to take a siesta in the shade. As with most land tortoises, its needs are very modest. It is almost completely herbivorous, feeding mainly on the softer leaves and shoots of shrubs, on grass and on any fruit it happens to find on the ground.

In March, when the tortoises wake from their winter sleep, they mate. A brief courtship is followed by copulation, during which the males make audible sounds. Otherwise, apart from snorts and snuffles, they are silent throughout their life. A few weeks after mating, the females dig shallow holes under the bushes, in which they lay a few round, hard-shelled eggs. Older females may produce as many as 10 eggs. The incubation period is 70 days. The newly-hatched young measure about 3 cm and are herbivorous like their parents.

Young marginated tortoises are a very dark colour or black. Older individuals (1) have a somewhat lighter carapace with rather indistinct markings. They differ from other members of the genus *Testudo* in respect of the markedly compressed, unmistakable hind part of their carapace. Young specimens display the same feature.

3

In the winter, when it is cold, the tortoises hibernate, but in the summer, when it is dry and hot and the vegetation withers, they likewise retire underground (2), hide among fallen leaves or crawl under stones.

In the United States the genus *Testudo* is replaced by the genus *Gopherus*. Here also is the home of the prettily marked box tortoises, such as the Ornate Box Turtle, *Terrapene ornata* (3), which is able to close its shell and so protect its head and forelimbs by snapping the anterior edge of its plastron shut against the edge of the carapace.

In Europe the species *Agrionemys horsfieldii* is occasionally encountered. It has four toes and comes mainly from the Caspian Sea region. Sometimes it escapes from captivity and sometimes, no longer wanted, it is released and left to fend for itself.

2

1

European Pond Terrapin
Emys orbicularis   Emydidae

Compared with other continents, Europe has very few freshwater chelonians. In fact, it has only two species — the European Pond Terrapin and the Stripe-necked Terrapin. The most northerly limits of the European Pond Terrapin are the German Democratic Republic, Poland and other Baltic countries. It inhabits the whole of southern Europe and in the east it occurs as far as the Sea of Aral, it is also to be found in north Africa and south-western Asia.

It is most likely to be encountered between April and October in warm still water, usually among dense aquatic vegetation, but it also lives in slow rivers, irrigation canals and marshes. It likes to bask in the sun on the water's edge, but it is very timid and the slightest disturbance sends it into hiding in the water. Its carapace can measure 30 cm and the animal may weigh 1 kg, but most specimens are smaller.

The male differs from the female in respect of its concave plastron and posteriorly wider carapace. The diet of this animal consists mainly of molluscs, worms and insects, but terrapins also eat small fishes and frogs.

The European Pond Terrapin is oviparous, the female laying up to 15 eggs measuring 30 × 40 mm in a dry, sandy spot not far from water. She digs a pit about 15 cm deep with her hind legs and after the eggs have been laid she carefully covers them over and smooths the earth down with her plastron. The duration of incubation depends on the temperature and 3—4 months of fairly high temperatures are usually needed. In cold, damp summers the embryos do not develop at all. In central Europe the young hatch in August or September. Their carapace is soft and about 2 cm long. They usually hibernate in the place where they were hatched, while the adult animals hibernate in mud at the bottom of a river or pond.

2

The shell of pond terrapins is very variably marked. It can be a plain colour, have small spots and dashes, or carry a regular pattern of radiating lines (1).

In Europe, the area of the Stripe-necked Terrapin, *Mauremys caspica,* consists of three isolated parts with distinct subspecies — *Mauremys caspica leprosa* on the Iberian Peninsula, *M. c. rivulata* (2) in the south of the Balkan Peninsula and the nominate subspecies, *M. c. caspica,* near the Caspian Sea. It has adapted itself to various environments and is to be found in mountain streams, in still water and in brackish water at the mouth of rivers.

Among the numerous species of freshwater chelonians inhabiting North America, many are brightly coloured (e. g. the genus *Chrysemys*) or have an exotic form. Such a one is the Snapper, *Chelydra serpentina,* of the family Chelydridae, which can weigh over 30 kg and measure 100 cm (3).

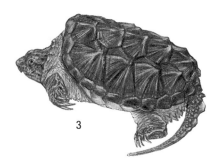

3

1

Leathery Turtle
Dermochelys coriacea
Dermochelyidae

The Leathery Turtle is a veritable giant, not only among chelonians, but among reptiles in general. This marine turtle normally measures 200 cm and weighs about 500 kg, but even larger specimens have been caught. For instance, one caught off Vancouver in Canada in 1931 weighed 652 kg, while the largest ever — caught in the Pacific — measured 230 cm and weighed 700 kg.

Two subspecies used to be differentiated — *Dermochelys coriacea coriacea* and *D. c. schlegeli,* but today most experts are agreed that *D. c. schlegeli* is only a synonym.

The Leathery Turtle is distributed all around the world, but is commonest in tropical seas. It has been found in the Pacific, the Atlantic and the Indian oceans and even (though rarely) in the Mediterranean. It lives mainly on fish, crustaceans and certain molluscs.

The females alone visit dry land, when they come to lay their eggs, and only a few places visited by them are known, but in May and June the turtles always make an appearance on the coast of the East Malaccan state of Trengganu. The eggs are about 53 mm in diameter and number 90 — 150. The female digs a pit in the sand, lays the eggs, covers them over and in about an hour is back in the sea. The young turtles hatch in 52 — 65 days, (usually at night), worm their way out of the sand and immediately make for the water. At this time they are easy prey for all kinds of predators, from birds of prey on the land to sharks in the water. In consequence, only one per cent ever reach adulthood.

The Leathery Turtle (1) is anatomically very different from other living chelonians. Its vertebrae and ribs are not fused with the carapace. The latter is composed of polygonal bony plates and, like the head and the limbs, is covered with a thick skin. The plastron is only leathery and in the young it has five longitudinal ridges. Leathery turtles are in general very flat and they have powerful oarlike forelegs which enable them to swim very quickly, while steering with their hind legs. One of their most striking features are the horny edges of their upper jaw, which, on either side, has three notches with a tooth in the middle.

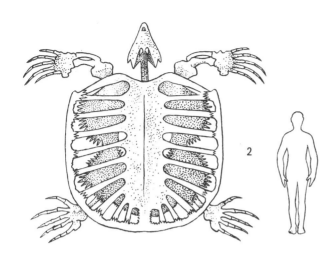

2

In bygone geological ages the seas were inhabited by even bigger chelonians. *Archelon ischyros* (2), which belonged to the family Protostegidae, lived in the Mesozoic era, 140—65 million years ago, was over 3 metres long and weighed up to 2 tonnes.

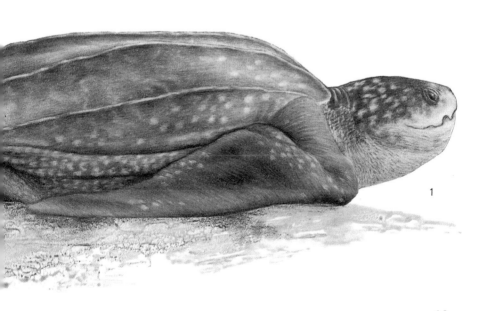

1

93

Loggerhead Turtle
Caretta caretta

Cheloniidae

Of all the marine turtles, the area of distribution of the Loggerhead Turtle reaches furthest north and several times it has been caught off the coast of Great Britain. The nominate subspecies, *Caretta caretta caretta,* inhabits the Mediterranean, the Black Sea and the Atlantic Ocean, while *C. c. gigas* (differentiated by the two claws on its fore-limbs) lives in the Pacific and Indian oceans.

The Loggerhead Turtle is one of the most abundant marine turtles, not only because of its wide geographical distribution and modest requirements as regards the temperature of the water, but chiefly because nobody is interested in it either for its flesh or its shell, and it is therefore not hunted as much as other species.

These predacious turtles feed mainly on molluscs and crustaceans, but also devour less nimble species of fish.

They breed in tropical seas and also in the Mediterranean. At night, the females lay their eggs in pits about 60 cm deep, which they dig out in a sandy shore. The eggs are 40 mm in diameter and number up to 150. Since the female lays them at a rate of 12 a minute, the whole egg-laying process does not take more than 10—15 minutes. When they have finished, the females cover the eggs with sand and quickly return to the sea. The young, which hatch in 30—60 days, measure about 5 cm and are dark brown to black in colour. As soon as they hatch they make for the sea, where they have the same diet as adult turtles. The newly-hatched turtles have conspicuously long, flat fore-limbs like flippers.

Many questions cencerning the biology of marine turtles are still partly or altogether unanswered — for instance, what regions and what depths they frequent during the year, how they find their way about, how the males and females come together to mate, how they communicate, etc. These questions are now studied by marking and the use of radio.

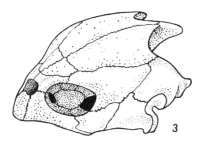

3

The Loggerhead Turtle has an average length of 100—130 cm and weighs about 150 kg, but still larger specimens are occasionally caught. In the collection at Cambridge University, for example, is the skull of a huge specimen the weight of which was estimated to have been about 500 kg, since the skull alone is almost 30 cm long. The skulls (3) are altogether very massive, with powerful jaws, so that the whole head gives the impression of being even more robust than that of other marine turtles.

Adult loggerhead turtles have a brown back, light-coloured limbs and a dark-spotted head (2). The plates of the carapace are contiguous and its posterior edge has coarse teeth like a saw. The plastron is a plain light brown (1).

Like all the other members of the Cheloniidae, the Loggerhead Turtle is unable to withdraw its head into its shell.

Kemp's Ridley
Lepidochelys kempii
Cheloniidae

The home of this turtle is far from the coast of Europe, in the tropical and subtropical waters of the Gulf of Mexico. Very occasionally it may be sighted in mid-Atlantic and, more rarely still, young specimens with carapaces measuring about 30 cm appear off the European coast.

Kemp's Ridley feeds partly on vegetable material, especially seaweed, but it does not despise either crabs or shrimps. For a long time it was not known where or how it reproduced, but in 1961 scientists heard of a sandy shore near Veracruz in Mexico, to which the turtles came in spring to lay their eggs. About 40,000 female turtles crawled out on to the fine sand to lay their eggs at a safe distance from the high tide mark. The scientists were very surprised to find that the eggs were laid during the daytime, since other marine turtles lay their eggs under the cover of darkness.

In 1966 a unique plan was drawn up to help protect rare marine turtles. Entitled 'Operation Padre', its purpose was to collect turtle eggs along the Mexican coast, where their safety was threatened by mankind as well as by coyotes, which devoured both the eggs and the newly-hatched turtles. Large numbers of young were saved in this way, as the eggs were taken to the safe shores of the uninhabited island of Padre, and so the turtles which were hatched on this island now return there to lay their own eggs.

Before they are released into the sea, the newly-hatched turtles are measured, weighed and marked. Marking serves the same purpose as in the case of birds, helping to trace the movements of turtles during the year and to determine their age, etc.

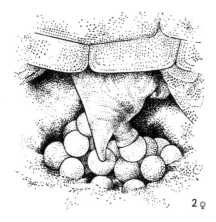

2 ♀

The carapace of adult specimens of Kemp's Ridley does not measure more than 80 cm, making this the smallest of the marine turtles (1). The female lays up to 100 round eggs in a pit which she has already dug in the sand with her hind legs, and then carefully covers them up again (2). The young turtles crawl out of the sand in about eight weeks and, guided by an infallible instinct, immediately make their way to the sea.

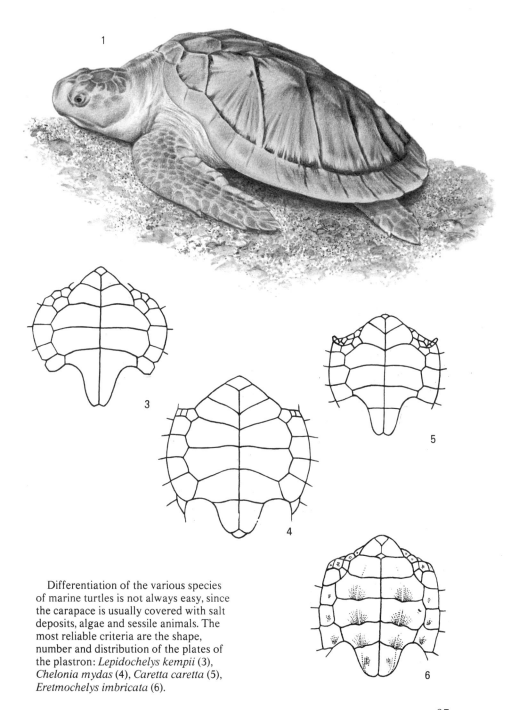

1

3

4

5

6

Differentiation of the various species of marine turtles is not always easy, since the carapace is usually covered with salt deposits, algae and sessile animals. The most reliable criteria are the shape, number and distribution of the plates of the plastron: *Lepidochelys kempii* (3), *Chelonia mydas* (4), *Caretta caretta* (5), *Eretmochelys imbricata* (6).

Green Turtle
Chelonia mydas

Cheloniidae

The Green Turtle is another marine species occasionally found off the coast of Europe. The nominate subspecies, *Chelonia mydas mydas,* inhabits the Mediterranean and the Atlantic, while *C. m. japonica* occurs mainly in the Indian and the Pacific oceans.

The Green Turtle is one of the largest of its kind, since it can attain a length of over 100 cm and weighs about 250 kg. The biggest specimen so far known measured 140 cm and weighed 450 kg. Despite their size — emphasized by their large, round head — these turtles are excellent swimmers and are often encountered in the open sea, far away from any land. They also sleep on the water, but the slightest interruption sends them diving down into the depths, where a single breath lasts them for about an hour. According to the literature, their maximum recorded swimming rate is 40 km an hour.

The Green Turtle has no pronounced hook at the tip of its jaws, which are finely serrated. It is herbivorous, feeding primarily on aquatic plants, and it has a special predilection for eel grass (*Zostera* spp.).

These turtles leave the sea only to lay their eggs. The female lays 75−200 eggs 40 mm in diameter, divided into 2−5 clutches over the course of the year. She buries them in fine sand on the shore and the young turtles hatch in 6−10 weeks. As soon as they have scrambled out of the sand they set out for the sea, instinctively guided by their vision (the surf is phosphorescent at night) and by the slope of the shore.

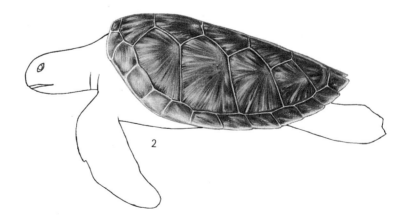

2

The Green Turtle (1) has very variable colouring, but is most commonly a dark brownish green with yellow spots and marbled markings. Its underside is yellow or a dingy white. The plates of the carapace (2) are contiguous and not overlapping. The head is so large that it cannot be withdrawn into the shell. The forelimbs are of the flipper type, like those of other marine turtles, and on each of them there is a single claw. The head and limbs of the young turtles are disproportionately large in relation to their body (3).

Adult green turtles have virtually no natural enemies, but the newly-hatched young are easy prey for beasts and birds of prey, especially eagles, while those which successfully reach the sea find predacious fishes and sharks waiting for them.

3

1

Hawksbill
Eretmochelys imbricata
Cheloniidae

The carapace of the Hawksbill Turtle is usually not more than 90 cm long. It is typical — especially in young specimens — for the plates of the carapace to overlap like roof tiles. This turtle inhabits a broad zone comprising all the warm seas of the world. The nominate subspecies, *Eretmochelys imbricata imbricata,* lives in the Atlantic and the subspecies *E. i. bissa* in the Pacific and Indian oceans. On very rare occasions the Hawksbill Turtle has been sighted off the coast of Great Britain and in the Mediterranean. It particularly likes shallow, sun-warmed bays, lagoons and even river mouths. It feeds mainly on flesh and the chief components of its diet are molluscs and crustaceans, although it is not above eating dead fish. Most of the females of the Atlantic population lay their eggs on the Panama coast. Each female produces 150—200 eggs, resembling ping-pong balls in size and appearance.

At one time the Hawksbill Turtle was in danger of becoming extinct. The plates of its carapace — 'tortoiseshell' — were used to make trinkets and utilitarian articles like combs. If warmed, tortoiseshell becomes pliable and easy to cut, grind and polish. Its characteristic feature is the light amber mottling against a dark background. It was the advent of cheap plastic materials that saved the turtle from extermination and it is interesting to note that many plastic articles are still coloured in such a way that they are indistinguishable from genuine tortoiseshell.

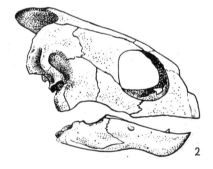

Like those of all marine turtles, the limbs of the Hawksbill Turtle (1) have adapted to become wide flippers and are too large to be withdrawn inside the shell. They have a classic skeleton (7) with five digits, however, and 1—3 claws protruding at the edge. The stronger forelimbs are used for swimming and the hind limbs for steering. The females also dig the pits for their eggs with their hind limbs.

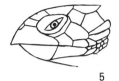

3 4 5 6

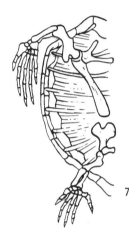

7

Marine turtles have robustly constructed skulls with hooked, toothless jaws (2). In place of teeth they have a horny, finely dentated plate no less efficient than genuine teeth. Features differentiating the Hawksbill Turtle from the Green Turtle are to be found on the heads of these animals. The former has a larger number of scales on the top of its head (3) and a markedly hooked upper jaw (5), while the latter has fewer scales on its head (4) and its jaws are less obviously hooked (6).

1

Moorish Gecko
Tarentola mauritanica   Gekkonidae

The Moorish Gecko can be encountered in the western part of the Mediterranean, on the Canary Islands and in north Africa from Morocco to Egypt. In Europe it occurs in Iberia, along the coasts of Dalmatia and Greece, and on Crete. Two subspecies have been described. The larger, *Tarentola mauritanica deserti*, lives in northern Africa and can be distinguished from *T. m. mauritanica* by its lighter colouring and markedly nocturnal mode of life.

The Moorish Gecko measures 12—16 cm and is the largest member of the family in Europe. It lives on the seashore or on islands, where it mainly frequents rocks and sun-warmed tree trunks. In spring it comes out of hiding in the morning, but in summer it is more often seen in the afternoon and evening. In more northerly regions it spends the winter resting in a crevice, under stones or in a hollow tree. It feeds on a variety of invertebrates and on rare occasions it attacks small vertebrates — not excluding its own young.

Mating takes place at the outset of spring, when the clear, clicking voice of the males can be heard in the afternoon and early evening. Toward the end of spring or in summer the females lay their eggs — usually two — which they make fast under stones or in cracks in the rocks. The eggs, which measure 13 × 10 mm, have a chalky shell. When they are first laid the shell is soft, but it hardens in a few hours. The young, which often do not hatch out for 4 months, are 3—5 cm long. After their first moult, when, like the parents, they eat the old skin, they catch small insects. Unlike adult geckos they have a boldly striped tail.

Apart from a few viviparous species in New Zealand, geckos lay just two eggs. These are at first soft and sticky and are easily attached to bark or a stone, but they soon grow harder in the air. When laying her eggs the female often uses her hind legs to assist the process.

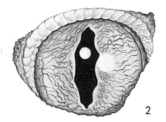

2

Like the Moorish Gecko (1), most geckos are territorial animals. That is to say, all their life they remain on one small patch of territory, which the males especially defend against intruders. As ones of the few vocal reptiles they utter various clicking and barking sounds.

Geckos are usually particularly lively after dusk or at night. During the daytime

102

3

4

1

their pupils are narrow (2), but as the light fades they dilate. The eyes are protected by transparent, fused lids.

Many geckos are able to climb over smooth vertical surfaces such as glass, even head downwards. This is because the underside of their toes is specially adapted (3 — *Tarentola mauritanica*, 4 — *Hemidactylus turcicus*). When they press their toes on the wall, the air is forced out of the spaces between the lamellae, converting them to suction pads. Furthermore, between the lamellae there are large numbers of microscopic bristles the hooked tips of which engage even the most minute cracks. Species which lack lamellae are unable to climb smooth surfaces.

Turkish Gecko
Hemidactylus turcicus
Gekkonidae

This gecko does not measure more than 10 cm and its skin is covered with prominent keeled scales. Its rather translucent pink skin creates an impression of fragility, especially in pregnant females, when the eggs can be seen gleaming through the abdominal skin.

The Turkish Gecko is most likely to be seen in the evening or at night, on the walls of stone buildings, in stone-terraced vineyards, on sunny rocks or under stones. It is interesting that, despite its nocturnal mode of life, it also appears at the entrance to its hiding-place during the daytime, to bask for a short time in the sun.

It feeds mainly on soft-bodied arthropods, such as spiders, and on dipterous insects. The males of this species can be traced by their clear, clicking sounds.

The females each lay two eggs and the young, which have a vividly striped tail, hatch in about two months.

The Turkish Gecko has a large area of distribution. It occurs throughout the whole of the Mediterranean region, including the islands of the Aegean and the northern coasts of Africa. It abounds on the shores of the Red Sea and extends southward into Kenya and eastward to India. It has even found its way to the United States and the islands of the Caribbean, since it frequents dockside warehouses as well as homes and hotels, from where it departs as a stowaway, nestling in the wrappings of various goods, in search of new worlds to conquer.

The majority of the 670 or so species of gecko are nocturnal or twilight animals and this accounts for the inconspicuous colouring of the Turkish Gecko (1). Bright colours are useless for communication in the dark and geckos have instead developed effective camouflage. There are, however, a few exceptions. For instance, the members of the genus *Phelsuma*, which inhabit Madagascar, have round pupils and bright colouring, but are vocally mute (Fig. 2 shows *Phelsuma cepediana*).

Geckos are unable to close their eyes, because during their evolution their eyelids fused and became transparent, as in snakes. If geckos need to wipe the dust from their eyes, they do so with their long tongue (3).

Kotschy's Gecko
Cyrtodactylus kotschyi

Gekkonidae

The range of Kotschy's Gecko comprises the southeast of the Balkan Peninsula, including the islands in the Aegean Sea, and south-eastern Italy. It has an isolated incidence on the Crimean coast and in the east stretches into south-eastern Asia. It forms 17 geographical races (sub-species) in the European part of its area of distribution and 7 others elsewhere.

The toes on the hind limbs of this gecko have a striking kink in them and scales on its tail are arranged in rings. If part of the tail is lost and grows again, the regenerated part is usually smooth and different in shape from the original structure.

Kotschy's Gecko is partly nocturnal in summer, but is active during the day in the cooler months, especially in the morning and evening. In the evenings, whole groups of them collect on the walls of old stone houses in the towns, in the light of the street lamps, rapidly devouring any small insects that come within reach, and they are often seen basking on cliffs in the late afternoon sunshine.

Three other species of geckos live along the eastern borders of Europe. One, the tiny *Cyrtodactylus russowii,* occurs in a single locality near the Caspian sea; *C. caspius,* which measures up to 16 cm, is found in several localities while the rarest of the three, the ground gecko *Alsophylax pipiens,* which lives in rodent burrows, utters clear ringing sounds like the call of a bird.

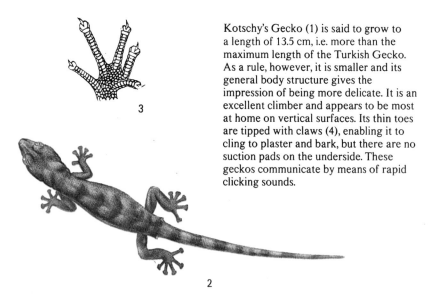

Kotschy's Gecko (1) is said to grow to a length of 13.5 cm, i.e. more than the maximum length of the Turkish Gecko. As a rule, however, it is smaller and its general body structure gives the impression of being more delicate. It is an excellent climber and appears to be most at home on vertical surfaces. Its thin toes are tipped with claws (4), enabling it to cling to plaster and bark, but there are no suction pads on the underside. These geckos communicate by means of rapid clicking sounds.

The European Leaf-toed Gecko, *Phyllodactylus europaeus*, (2) lives on many islands in the Tyrrhenian Sea, on Corsica, on Sardinia and on the islands along the Tunisian coast and on a small stretch of coast in north-western Italy. Its toes are very unusual in that they have lamellae, in the form of a forked pad, only at the tip, with a sharp claw protruding in the middle (3).

4

1

Hardun, Sling-tailed Agama
Agama stellio   Agamidae

Agamas are the Old World counterpart of the iguanas. In Europe, however, they are scarce, and of the 60 species of *Agama,* only three occur there.

The Hardun measures 30 cm together with the tail. Two subspecies inhabit the coasts of the Mediterranean countries. The nominate form, *Agama stellio stellio,* has been found in Europe on Corfu, on some of the Cyclades, on the island of Rhodes and in mainland Greece, chiefly in the neighbourhood of Salamis.

The Hardun loves sunshine and mainly inhabits sun-bathed cliffs, but it also frequents cultivated country, where it is to be found on stone walls, old buildings, or piles of stones. It can likewise climb trees very nimbly in search of the sun. It is very timid, however, and at the slightest sign of danger it rushes into hiding in a heap of stones or in a rodent burrow.

In June the female lays 6—14 eggs with leathery shells in shallow depression beside or under stones. In their natural environment, the young, which are about 4 cm long, hatch in August or at the beginning of September.

The toad-headed agamas (*Phrynocephalus*) are another type which can be found in eastern Europe. They are characterized by a large head and a noticeably flattened, smooth body. The three species which can be counted among the fauna of Europe — *P. helioscopus, P. guttatus* and *P. mystaceus* inhabit steppes and barren wastes with sandy ground. All of them live on insects.

2

1

The Hardun (1) is able, to some extent, to change colour, particularly the male. The front of his body turns red when he is excited.

The Caucasian Agama, *Agama caucasica* (2), which sometimes measures over 30 cm, lives in mountainous regions at altitudes up to 3,000 metres. Like the preceding species, it catches a variety of invertebrates and small vertebrates and occasionally eats plant material. It is also an excellent climber, making use both of the sharp claws on its toes and the keeled scales on its tail (3).

The last species which extends into Europe is *A. agilis sanguinolenta*. Its biology is the same as that of the other species, but it is much more brightly coloured.

3

Mediterranean Chameleon
Chamaeleo chamaeleon
Chamaeleontidae

No lizard has caught the imagination of the public as has the chameleon, with its many unique characteristics. For example, no other reptile can compete with it in the art of changing colour. This is determined by visual stimuli, the mood of the animal and the temperature of the environment. The process is brought about by chromatophores — cells containing various types of pigment granules. These are either scattered in the cell, or are concentrated together to form indefinite points of colour, making the colouring of the animal more vivid or paler, as the case may be. Chameleons have a laterally flattened body, but processes on their lungs allow it to be suddenly inflated to impress an enemy. Their eyes, which can be moved independently of each other, have fused, scaly lids, with a small opening in the middle. If the eyes face in the same direction, the chameleon sees things stereoscopically, but it can also observe two views at once. Its limbs are both striking and practical. Two and three digits respectively are fused down to the last joint and the resultant pincer-like organ, together with the prehensile tail, is invaluable for maintaining a hold on branches and twigs. The chameleon also approaches its prey with characteristic movements, swaying slowly backwards and forwards so that it looks like a large leaf. It does not display obvious sexual dimorphism.

Three subspecies of the Mediterranean Chameleon inhabit the Mediterranean region (a fourth lives in India). The nominate subspecies, the European Chameleon, *Chamaeleo chamaeleon chamaeleon,* is found in scrub country in the European part of this region. These typically diurnal animals spend most of their life on bushes and trees, but in the late summer the females come down to the ground. Here they each lay 30 or so eggs at the foot of a tree, and cover them with soil. The young hatch out in the following spring.

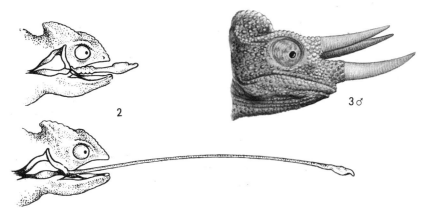

2

3 ♂

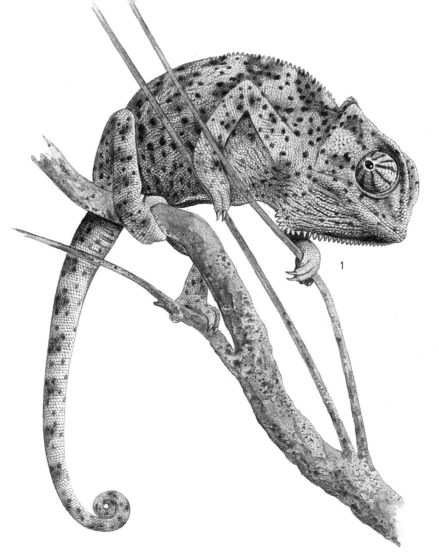

The Mediterranean Chameleon (1) attains a length of 20 – 30 cm. It is a harmless animal, its only defence being perfect colour camouflage and sluggishness, both of which make it hard to detect. It lives primarily on insects, catching them with its sticky tongue, which can be extended (2) to a distance equal to the length of its body. When not in use, the tongue lies coiled up on the floor of the mouth. When it is shot out, the widened end curls round the prey and draws it into the mouth, where it is crushed by the strong jaws and then swallowed. Chameleons have excellent sight and use it to locate their prey.

Except for the Mediterranean Chameleon, all 80 or so species of this family live in Africa. Some species, such as Jackson's Chameleon, *C. jacksonii* (3), have menacing horns on their heads which deter their enemies, while others have helmets or crests.

Dalmatian Algyroides
Algyroides nigropunctatus   Lacertidae

The genus *Algyroides* is distinguished from the members of the genus *Lacerta* by the markedly ridged scales on the back and tail, which partly overlap each other. Africa is the principal home of this genus but four species, all very similar, have spread to the most southerly parts of Europe.

The Dalmatian Algyroides, measuring up to 21 cm, and with a tail double the length of its body, is the largest of these. It also inhabits the largest area, which comprises the coasts of Yugoslavia, Albania and Greece, and in some places it penetrates inland. In Italy it lives in a small region near Trieste.

This lizard frequents scrubland with evergreen vegetation, loose stone walls, terraced vineyards and ruins (where it also hibernates) and it sometimes even appears in gardens. It climbs walls, bushes and trees with great agility.

It mates soon after emerging from hibernation, generally in April, when the males have a vivid blue throat and an orange-red belly. In May the females lay two (rarely three) eggs, and it is thought likely that some have two reproductive cycles a year, since egg-bearing females have been observed in late summer.

In the spring and autumn the lizards can be seen throughout the day, but at the height of summer they shelter from the noonday heat in the shade of vegetation or under stones.

The members of the genus *Algyroides* (especially the other three species) are the smallest representatives of the Lacertidae family in Europe.

The shape of the body of the Dalmatian Algyroides (1) as well as its size and habits are reminiscent of the Wall Lizard. A close view shows the large, diagonally ridged scales (2).

Algyroides moreoticus, which has a body 5 cm long, occurs in southern Greece and on some of the Greek islands. It has a less brightly coloured belly than the preceding species and the female has

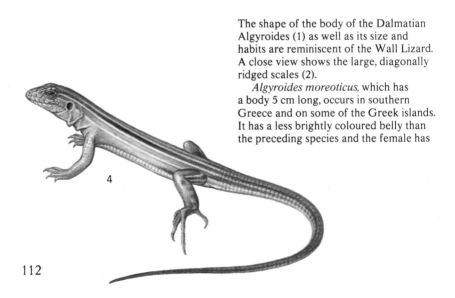

4

1

2

3

light spots on her sides. *A. fitzingeri,*
which is even smaller, lives on Corsica
and Sardinia, while *A. marchi* was
described in 1958 in a small, localized
area of south-eastern Spain. The map (3)
illustrates the disjointed distribution of
the genus *Algyroides.*

In North America, the Old World
family Lacertidae is replaced by the small
members of the Teidae family
(Fig. 4 shows the Six-lined Lizard or
Race-runner, *Cnemidophorus
sexlineatus*).

113

Snake-eyed Lizard
Ophisops elegans

Lacertidae

Five species of the genus *Ophisops* live in the steppes of western Asia and in north-eastern Africa, but only one is found in Europe. Small populations of the Snake-eyed Lizard are found in Transcaucasia and in the south-eastern part of the Balkan Peninsula, where it occurs near the Bulgarian town of Svilengrad.

It leaves its winter shelter very early — often at the end of February, when it can be seen on clay or stony slopes, on sun-warmed hillsides with plenty of bushes, in open deciduous woods or in vineyards. Anyone who has had an opportunity of observing this interesting lizard in its natural surroundings will have been surprised at its curious behaviour. When disturbed, it does not make for the nearest shelter, but runs from one clump of grass to the next, or from one stone to another, climbs on top of it and looks round to find the intruder. If the lizard is left in peace for a little while, it then stands on its hind legs, supported by its tail, and 'begs', turning its head briskly from side to side and waving its forelimbs in the air. These lizards have been seen to rear up and run a short distance on their hind legs.

The female lays 4 or 5 eggs twice a year and since egg-bearing females have still been encountered late in the summer, experts are of the opinion that they sometimes lay a third batch. The young have conspicuous longitudinal stripes.

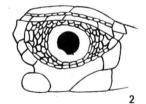

2

Adult snake-eyed lizards can be distinguished from young ones by their more spotted body (1). As their name implies, they have eyes like those of a snake. This is an interesting adaptation among European lizards. During evolution, the lower lid gradually covered the whole eye and united with the upper lid. Afterward this, a transparent, rounded 'window' developed in them (2, 3). The lids remain capable of movement over the eyeball, however, and partial closure of the eye can be brought about by a downward and obliquely backward shift of the upper part.

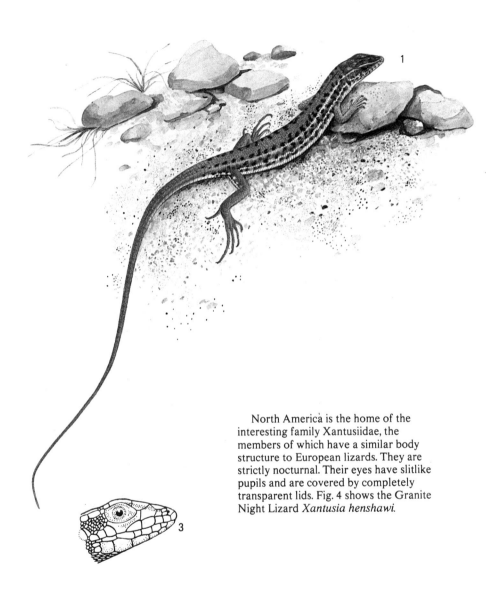

North America is the home of the
interesting family Xantusiidae, the
members of which have a similar body
structure to European lizards. They are
strictly nocturnal. Their eyes have slitlike
pupils and are covered by completely
transparent lids. Fig. 4 shows the Granite
Night Lizard *Xantusia henshawi.*

Large Psammodromus
Psammodromus algirus
Lacertidae

This lizard utters shrill whistles when it is picked up. When released a little, it wriggles free and disappears with great rapidity into a clump of grass or beneath a stone.

The Large Psammodromus lives in very sunny, stony localities with sparse vegetation not requiring much moisture, but it often appears in the immediate vicinity of human dwellings, sunning itself on fences. It inhabits the northwest coast of Africa and the nominate subspecies also occurs in the south of France and the Iberian Peninsula.

Its long, slim, cylindrical body is covered with strikingly large rhomboid, keeled scales, which overlap each other along the back of the animal. The long, fragile tail accounts for almost three quarters of the total length of this lizard. The males which are usually larger have one or two bright blue, luminous, dark-edged spots on their shoulders, and breeding males have a red throat and red cheeks. The females have no red colouring and usually have two less intensely coloured blue spots.

These lizards feed on various small insects and spiders, which they catch on the run. They hibernate in holes and in crevices in stone walls. Mating takes place in April or May and in May the females lay 8−11 eggs, from which the young hatch in July or August. The young, which have the same colouring as the adult lizards, catch small insects and insect larvae.

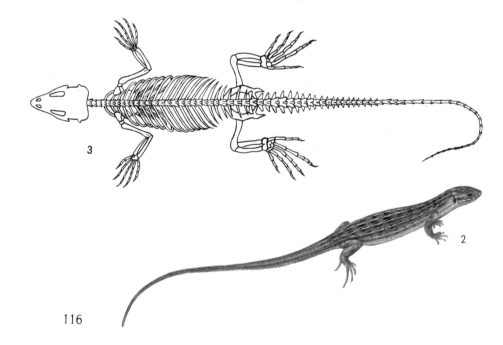

3

2

1

4

5

The Large Psammodromus (1) attains
a length of 20—27 cm (including the long
tail) and is the largest of the 12 members
of this genus.

Another European species, the
Spanish Sand Racer, *Psammodromus
hispanicus* (2), which also forms two
subspecies, lives in the south of France
and the Iberian Peninsula. It is
substantially smaller and only measures
up to 12 cm. Its biology is similar to that
of the preceding species. It also lives in
dry localities and is often seen on sandy
seashores. The two species differ in the
shape of scales in the throat region:
P. algirus (4) and *P. hispanicus* (5).

All the members of the Lacertidae
have a completely ossified skeleton (3)
and well-developed limbs. Their teeth are
attached to the inner edge of their jaws.

Fringe-fingered Lizard
Acanthodactylus erythrurus
Lacertidae

The Fringe-fingered Lizard, which is over 20 cm long, is the only member of the genus *Acanthodactylus* found in Europe. The 18 species of the genus are distributed over a wide arid belt which crosses the Iberian Peninsula, north Africa and western Asia to India. The incidence of the Fringe-fingered Lizard in Europe is limited to Spain and Portugal, and even there it is found only on sandy ground. This lizard can tolerate extreme heat and it not only frequents sunny spots, but it often runs over the surface of hot sand with a temperature of 50 °C and over. If there are stones lying about on the sand, it shelters beneath them. It also digs burrows for itself in the dunes, or occupies the burrows of small mammals.

This exceedingly timid lizard can run very quickly. The plates on its digits have lateral projections forming fine fringes, which play a very useful role in preventing the limbs from sinking into fine, loose sand.

Females up to the age of 3 years lay 4—6 eggs only once a year, but older females lay eggs twice a year. In Europe the first clutch is laid at the end of May or the beginning of June and the second at the end of July or the beginning of August. The brightly coloured young, measuring about 6 cm, hatch after 70—75 days of incubation in hot sand. Like other lizards, this species has many enemies, including reptilian predators such as the Ocellated Lizard, the Southern Smooth Snake, the Montpelier Snake and Lataste's Viper.

The gaudy markings on the back of the adult Fringe-fingered Lizard (1) and the young (2) are the best possible camouflage in the shadows thrown by the blades of grasses which grow in its sandy habitats. In the females and young, the underside of the tail is a vivid crimson.

Observations in the wild and in captivity have shown that the optimum temperatures for most lizards of the warm European south are 20—30 °C, and higher temperatures can be tolerated for only a short time. Temperature also regulates the diurnal activity of lizards. In

2

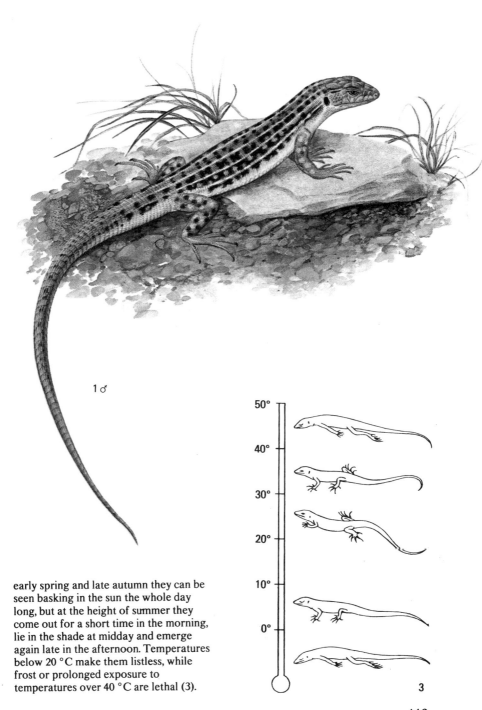

1 ♂

early spring and late autumn they can be seen basking in the sun the whole day long, but at the height of summer they come out for a short time in the morning, lie in the shade at midday and emerge again late in the afternoon. Temperatures below 20 °C make them listless, while frost or prolonged exposure to temperatures over 40 °C are lethal (3).

50°
40°
30°
20°
10°
0°

3

Racerunner, Desert Lacertid
Eremias arguta
Lacertidae

This moderately large lizard differs from European species of the genus *Lacerta* in having a pointed snout and a tail which suddenly narrows after the first third. Further morphological characters also mark it as one of the many steppe and desert lizards originating in centres in Asia and Africa. This racerunner is distributed from Mongolia across central Asia and the Caucasus to the delta of the Danube in Rumania. It frequents only sandy ground and since there are no spreading steppes or deserts in the most western part of its area, it colonizes sandy regions on the coasts or on river banks. Quite often it even settles on isolated patches of dry, sandy ground in the middle of marshes.

It shelters under stones or digs itself a burrow about half a metre long beneath clumps of tall grass, and here it also hibernates from September or October, according to the weather, emerging in March or by the middle of April. Beetles, ants, spiders and even small snails form its diet. Mating takes place in April and the female lays 3—11 eggs about 16 mm long. The young which measure about 6 cm hatch out in about two months.

Some time ago an interesting rescue operation was carried out in Rumania. When the habitats of this rare lizard were to be flooded to make way for a reservoir, a large part of the population was caught and taken to places not endangered by technical progress. Five subspecies have been described in all, two of which live in Europe. *E. arguta deserti* is distributed from Rumania to Azerbaijan and *E. a. transcaucasica* occurs in Transcaucasia.

Another racerunner which extends from the east to the Volga basin and the western shore of the Caspian Sea forms a specific subspecies — *E. velox caucasica* — exactly in the European part of this area.

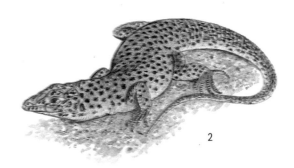

2

With its robust head and powerful jaws,
an adult specimen of *Eremias arguta* (1)
can crush the hard wing cases of large
beetles.

Certain typical desert species from the
more arid parts of Asia, such as the desert
lacertid *E. grammica* (2), are interesting.
Their thin digits are equipped with
fringed processes which treble the area of
their toes, thereby preventing them from
sinking into the fine sand (3 — a whole
toe, 4 — a detail of one segment). In the
Kyzylkum desert, in the burning noonday
heat, these lizards escape from the hot
sand to the branches of saxaul trees to
cool themselves.

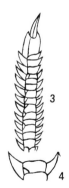

Ocellated Lizard
Lacerta lepida

Lacertidae

For every zoologist it is exciting to come across an Ocellated Lizard, since it is the largest member of the Lacertidae, as well as the largest lizard in Europe. The brightly coloured males, which are larger than the females, have a total length of 50—60 cm, although still larger individuals are caught from time to time (the largest known specimen measured a full 90 cm, together with its tail).

Because of its size, this lizard needs something more substantial to eat than just insects and other invertebrates. In the spring it takes young birds from their nests, devours small rodents and catches small reptiles, including snakes. In the summer it enriches its diet with fallen fruit.

With three subspecies it inhabits the western part of the Mediterranean region, where it has been found in Spain, Portugal, the south of France, north-western Italy and the coast of north-west Africa. Its northern limits roughly coincide with the distribution of olive trees. It inhabits a wide range of habitats up to an altitude of 1,000 metres in the Alps and 2,100 metres in the Pyrenees, but it prefers dry localities overgrown with shrubs, old vineyards and deserted orchards and olive groves, where it finds sufficient food and good hiding-places. It shelters mainly in abandoned rodent burrows, or in old trees with hollow trunks. Despite its size it is a fast runner and nimble climber.

The adult male Ocellated Lizard (1) differs from the female in being generally larger and more gaudy in appearance. In addition to a bright green body, the males have three or four rows of large blue spots, ringed with black, down their sides. The females are generally only brown, with mere traces of spots. The size of this lizard is emphasized by the robust body and massive head, which is covered with large scales (2).

3

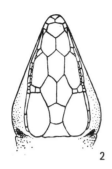

Ocellated lizards begin to hibernate in October and wake in February or March. Their eggs are laid during April and May and clutches of over twenty are by no means rare. Like those of all oviparous lizards, the eggs have an elastic, parchment-like shell. The female buries them in soil between stones or under the roots of a tree and the young, which measure about 6 cm, hatch in less than three months. The young (3) have different colouring from their parents. In the wild they live for about 5 years, but in captivity have been known to attain a maximum age of 11 years.

2

1 ♂

Green Lizard
Lacerta viridis
Lacertidae

This attractively coloured lizard is found in several subspecies distributed over large parts of Europe. In the west its area stretches to the north of Spain and the Atlantic coast of France, while in the east it extends to the River Dnieper. It also occurs in Turkey, the Balkan Peninsula, Italy and Sicily. In the north its incidence coincides with the vine-growing regions and in Czechoslovakia it spreads northward along rocky river valleys warmed by the sun. Its most northerly recorded incidence is in the German Democratic Republic, Holland and Poland. In the mountains of southern Europe it ascends to an altitude of 1,800 metres.

The Green Lizard, which with the tail measures up to 40 cm, is the largest lizard of central Europe.

This lizard makes its spring appearance in April and the breeding season lasts until June. About six weeks after mating the female lays 8—20 white eggs and buries them in pits dug in the ground. The young, which measure about 4 cm, hatch in August or September and immediately set about catching insects. Their hibernation begins later than in the adult animals and if the weather is mild, they can often still be seen at the end of October. They become sexually mature after three years.

Green lizards frequent rocky steppes, pastures and wooded steppes. They are excellent climbers. If the weather is warm they can be seen all day long. When in danger, they rush to the top of a tree or vanish into a deep burrow. Throughout most of Europe the Green Lizard is protected by law, but in many places the use of chemicals in forestry has caused its populations to dwindle.

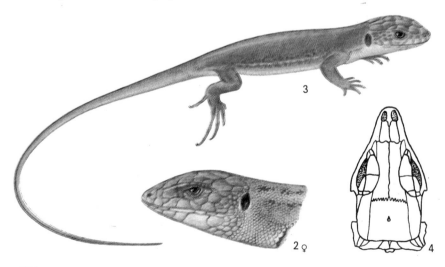

3

2 ♀

4

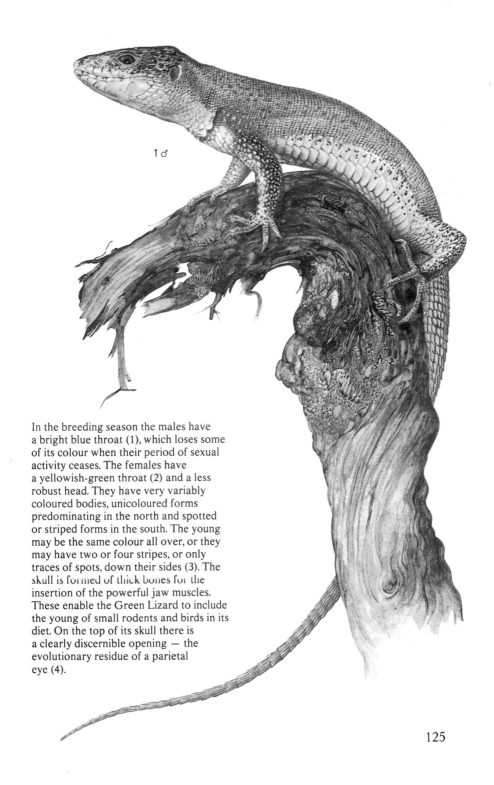

1 ♂

In the breeding season the males have a bright blue throat (1), which loses some of its colour when their period of sexual activity ceases. The females have a yellowish-green throat (2) and a less robust head. They have very variably coloured bodies, unicoloured forms predominating in the north and spotted or striped forms in the south. The young may be the same colour all over, or they may have two or four stripes, or only traces of spots, down their sides (3). The skull is formed of thick bones for the insertion of the powerful jaw muscles. These enable the Green Lizard to include the young of small rodents and birds in its diet. On the top of its skull there is a clearly discernible opening — the evolutionary residue of a parietal eye (4).

Balkan Green Lizard
Lacerta trilineata
Lacertidae

The Balkan Green Lizard, another large species with a total length of up to 50 cm, inhabits the Balkan Peninsula, the adjoining islands and western Asia. Five species are differentiated in the European part of its distribution area. *Lacerta trilineata trilineata* inhabits the Balkans, the Ionian Islands and Asia Minor, *L. t. dobrogica* north-western Bulgaria, *L. t. hansschweizeri* the islands of Milos, Kimolos and Sifnos and *L. t. polylepidota* Crete and Kithira, while *L. t. media* occurs from the north-eastern part of Asia Minor and across the Caucasus to the northern part of Mesopotamia. Nine other subspecies live in Asia.

The Balkan Green Lizard occurs mainly in lowlands, avoids mountains and is found only exceptionally at altitudes up to 1,000 metres. It frequents the same localities as other green species and like them is an expert climber of trees and bushes. Its period of hibernation and its diet are also similar. It catches small vertebrates and insects, and occasionally eats sweet fallen fruit.

Mating takes place in April. In mid-May the female lays 9—18 eggs measuring about 9 × 17 mm, and buries them in the ground. In the south she may lay a second clutch in the middle of June. The newly-hatched lizard (minus the tail) is 2.9—3.5 cm long. Sexual maturity is reached after two years, when the male measures at least 9.5 cm and the female 9 cm.

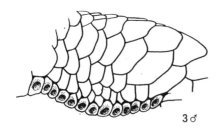

3 ♂

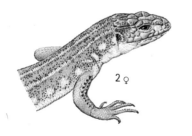

2 ♀

It is easy to determine the sex of the Balkan Green Lizard. The males (1) have a larger head and are plain green, with no markings, while the females (2) have light spots on their sides and pronounced whitish stripes running from the back of the head to the base of the tail. The young, which are similarly striped, can be distinguished from young green lizards by the number of light stripes. Young Balkan green lizards always have an odd number (3 or 5) and young green lizards an even number (2 or 4). It is the three dorsal stripes which give this species its Latin name, since the first scientific description was based on an immature animal.

1 ♂

The sex of all members of the
Lacertidae can also be determined from
the femoral pores (3) on the hind legs of
the males. These are most pronounced
during the breeding season.

Schreiber's Green Lizard
Lacerta schreiberi
Lacertidae

This is one of the large Lacertidae species with limited distribution. It measures about 30 cm (the body and head about 12 cm). It closely resembles the Ocellated Lizard and like it, has a robust body and massive head.

It occurs only in the north-western, western and southern part of the Iberian Peninsula. In the south it ascends to altitudes of up to 1,800 metres, but in the north it keeps to lower altitudes. Its habitats are similar to those of the Green Lizard — sunny hillsides overgrown with shrubs, dry roadsides and warm rocks. No subspecies have so far been described, although colour variants are known to exist. As distinct from the adult animals, the young have pronounced white spots on their sides.

Like all large lizards, this species catches small vertebrates as well as insects and occasionally eats ripe fruit which has fallen to the ground.

Lacerta strigata, which inhabits eastern Europe, the mountains of the Caucasus, the south-eastern shores of the Caspian Sea and Iran, Iraq and Asia Minor, is another large lizard. It has light longitudinal stripes on a greenish background. It inhabits the same kind of areas as the preceding species and in the mountains it occurs up to 2,500 metres. It feeds mainly on locusts. In the more southerly part of its area the females lay eggs twice a year, each clutch usually comprising 6 — 11 eggs measuring 9 × 16 mm. The young, which hatch in 60 days, measure about 6 cm. They attain sexual maturity after two years.

3

2 ♂

Schreiber's Green Lizard is characterized by marked dichroism. The males (2) have dark spots on a green background and a blue throat, while the females are brown and densely spotted, and their colouring is less variable (1).

The Moroccan Rock Lizard, *Lacerta perspicillata* (3), originally lived only in the mountains of north Africa, but it has since been introduced to the island of Minorca. It measures 14—18 cm, including the tail. This swift little lizard is remarkable for the transparent scale on its lower eyelid which differentiates it from all other species.

As with most lizards, fertilization takes place internally. The animals usually mate in spring. After a brief courtship the male, during copulation, seizes the female with his jaws and clasps her with his hind limbs (4).

1 ♀

4

Sand Lizard
Lacerta agilis
Lacertidae

The Sand Lizard inhabits the whole of Europe except the Mediterranean region, Ireland and northern Scandinavia. In the east it extends to Transcaucasia and continues, via the temperate belt of Asia, to Lake Baikal. In central Europe it is the best known and most common member of the Lacertidae. Its wide distribution is due largely to the fact that it is tolerant of a wide range of conditions, even finding good conditions for existence in the immediate vicinity of human dwellings. It is more abundant on the outskirts of forests and on heaths, although large populations also live on sunny railway embankments, etc. While preferring low altitudes, nevertheless it sometimes ascends high into the mountains, and has been found at an altitude of 3,500 metres. The Sand Lizard has strong territorial instincts and pairs or single individuals will occupy, mark and defend a limited area as their own, where they hunt, seek shelter and lay their eggs for years.

In the temperate belt the Sand Lizard hibernates from October to March or April. On waking it feeds voraciously, mainly on insects. Then, after about two moults, it assumes its typical colouring and seeks a mate. The female lays 5—15 eggs in early summer and the tiny young lizards hatch out in about five weeks.

On warm days these lizards are most active in the morning and late afternoon. Like most reptiles, if the weather is either cold or very hot they retire to their shelters.

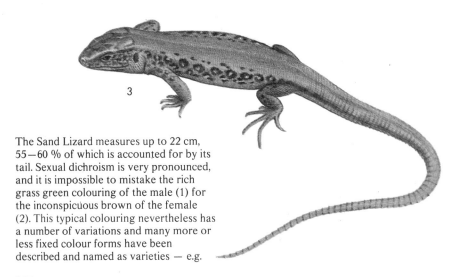

3

The Sand Lizard measures up to 22 cm, 55—60 % of which is accounted for by its tail. Sexual dichroism is very pronounced, and it is impossible to mistake the rich grass green colouring of the male (1) for the inconspicuous brown of the female (2). This typical colouring nevertheless has a number of variations and many more or less fixed colour forms have been described and named as varieties — e.g.

130

2 ♀

1 ♂

var. *erythronota* (3). The varieties also display sexual dichroism, however, so that males and females are still clearly distinguishable from each other.

Owing to its large distribution area, the Sand Lizard has many subspecies, differing chiefly as regards the arrangement of the scales on their head.

Although it is still the most abundant lizard in most parts of Europe, its populations are becoming steadily smaller. The main reasons for this are a high building rate, the salvaging of unproductive land for agriculture, the increasing popularity of nature for recreation purposes and the use of chemical poisons. The number of sand lizards is also kept down by pheasants, larger lizards, kestrels and chickens, domestic geese and cats.

Viviparous Lizard
Lacerta vivipara
Lacertidae

This tiny lizard is encountered in quite different ecosystems from those of other members of the family. It prefers damp habitats, such as peat-bogs, forest clearings, marshy meadows and moors. It even enters water, either voluntarily, or to escape from enemies, and it is a good swimmer. The Viviparous Lizard is distributed over almost the whole of Europe up to latitude 70° North, including the British Isles, and extends right across Siberia as far as Sakhalin. In the south of its range it becomes progressively more montane, and it has actually been recorded at an altitude of 3,500 metres.

Lacerta vivipara pannonica is a subspecies recently described in the lowlands of eastern Slovakia. It is probably a population descended from individuals washed down in the past from higher altitudes by floods.

The Viviparous Lizard must pay for its penetration to high latitudes (sometimes beyond the Arctic circle) by a long winter sleep, which, in the north, can last up to nine months. Conversely, in southern Europe it lasts only three months. Ovoviviparity is another form of adaptation to harsh conditions. The fertilized eggs, without a tough shell, remain in the body of the female and are not laid until embryogenesis has been completed. The young lizards (about 12) then pop out of the transparent membrane which is their only wrapping soon or immediately after the eggs have been laid. At birth the lizards measure about 4 cm.

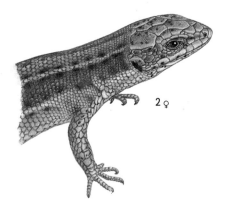

2 ♀

An adult Viviparous Lizard can measure up to 18 cm, but as a rule it is smaller. 60 % of its total length is accounted for by its tail. It is usually a very inconspicuous brownish-grey colour, with dark longitudinal stripes. Very dark or black (melanistic) individuals are occasionally found. The males (1) can be distinguished from the generally smaller females (2) by their vivid orange, dark-spotted belly (3).

1 ♂

3 ♂

In addition to small insects and spiders, viviparous lizards also feed on various worms, which abound in their damp habitats. The tiny young catch aphids and other small invertebrates. In central European latitudes they attain sexual maturity after three years, but further north the maturation process takes longer.

Wall Lizard
Podarcis muralis

Lacertidae

The Wall Lizard is an elegant, slender lizard with a long, whip-like tail. It measures 15—20 cm, about 60 % of which is accounted for by the tail.

This lizard runs nimbly over vertical rock faces, ruins and walls making characteristic jerky movements. It is even common in towns and gives tourists added pleasure as it enlivens the remains of historic buildings. In its localities it forms small communities. The Wall Lizard inhabits the greater part of Europe, with the exception of Great Britain, Poland and Scandinavia. It always frequents localities with a warm microclimate, preferably in lowlands, and is found in only a few places at altitudes up to 1,000 metres. Rocks or buildings are an essential part of its environment and it is evidently owing to the fact that sun-warmed walls hold the heat that the Wall Lizard can still be encountered at the end of autumn and the beginning of winter, or in February, if the sun is warm enough. It hibernates in deep chinks in walls and in rock crevices.

During the summer the female lays two or three clutches of 2—8 eggs with parchment-like shells, depositing them in cracks in the rocks or under stones. The young hatch in August and immediately begin an active search for food. They measure about 6 cm. Cannibalism is frequent among wall lizards.

2

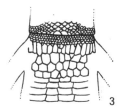

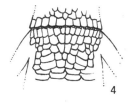

The Wall Lizard is very variably coloured and, what is more important, it displays great variability of form. About twenty subspecies have been described so far. In all the subspecies the males have a brick red belly and blue-spotted sides. Black (melanistic) individuals are frequent. Populations in the region around Rome contain brightly coloured males with a grass green, black-mottled back.

The subspecies *Podarcis muralis muralis* (1) occurs in central Europe. It likes to climb sheer walls (2) and is very nimble — a characteristic which makes it easy to identify.

The most reliable morphological differential character is the collar, which is straight-edged in the Wall Lizard (3) and has a serrated edge in the Sand Lizard and the Viviparous Lizard (4).

Ibiza Wall Lizard
Podarcis pityusensis   Lacertidae

The little-known Ibiza Wall Lizard is to be found only on the islands of Ibiza, Formentera and perhaps a few others in the Balearic group. It has also been introduced to Majorca. This slim-bodied, agile lizard often inhabits very inhospitable places. It is true that it also lives near human habitations where it chiefly frequents neglected gardens, rubbish dumps and waste ground, but it is mainly to be seen — especially on the smaller islands — beside the sea, on completely bare, sun-baked rocks on which no vegetation could ever survive.

Lilford's Wall Lizard, *Podarcis lilfordi,* similar to the Ibiza Wall Lizard in both size and appearance, also inhabits the Balearic Islands. Its body, together with the head, measures up to 8 cm and if tail is added, a maximum length is attained of 20 cm. This lizard also inhabits various inhospitable places and it is so modest in its requirements that it will even make do with a bare rock projecting from the sea. Thirteen subspecies have so far been found, each occupying only a very minute area. The nominate subspecies has been found only on Isla del Aire, a small island to the south-east of Minorca.

Both the above lizards eat insects and other small invertebrates, but the hard conditions under which they live drive them to accept plant material also, or to comb rubbish heaps for scraps.

Despite the remarkably variable colouring of the Ibiza Wall Lizard, two main types can be distinguished, which occur in separate localities. The ground colour on the back of lizards belonging to the population of the island of Formentera is green and they have brownish-grey sides (1), while specimens from the island of Ibiza have a brown back, reddish sides and more pronounced longitudinal rows of spots. Both types have a yellow to orange underside.

Lilford's Wall Lizard (2) is also variable in colour. Its back is usually green and its sides orange and spotted. Arrangement of the spots in longitudinal stripes is indistinct. Some individuals may be very dark or black, in which case the blue spots on their sides and throat stand out prominently against the black background (2).

137

Italian Wall Lizard
Podarcis sicula

Lacertidae

If a zoologist is given the task of identifying this pretty lizard, he is not entirely enthusiastic, since 40 different subspecies are already known — a most exceptional situation among vertebrates. The Italian Wall Lizard inhabits Corsica, Sardinia, Sicily, Italy, the western part of the Balkan Peninsula and the adjacent islands and the European part of Turkey. Small populations have also been found in south-eastern Spain and even in western Philadelphia in the United States, although in the last case the animals obviously found their way there through the agency of man.

These lizards usually occur in flat country at low altitudes, but isolated specimens have been found at altitudes up to 1,200 metres. They love the sun and sun-warmed spots are inhabited by large groups of them. They are not as timid as most lizards and can be seen near village buildings .where they know they can find enough food. They feed mainly on insects.

At the outset of spring, the males engage in fierce fights for the females, and in early summer the females lay 4 — 8 eggs, from which the young lizards hatch in about six weeks.

The Sicilian Wall Lizard, *Podarcis wagleriana,* is less variable. Of its three subspecies, *P. w. wagleriana* lives on the island of Sicily and the adjacent islands of Favignana and Levanzo, *P. w. antoninoi* on Vulcano and *P. w. marettimensis* on Marettimo.

2

The Italian Wall Lizard (1) can measure up to 25 cm (its body alone 9 cm), but it is usually much smaller.

The Sicilian Wall Lizard (2) is the same size. It also dwells on the plains, where it frequents warm, sunny, grassy spots not shaded by too much vegetation.

Members of the Lacertidae shed their skin several times a year (3). The old upper layer absorbs moisture from the surroundings, is detached from the underlying new layer, breaks away and is peeled off in strips. The lizard uses its jaws and hind limbs to accelerate the process and rubs itself against nearby objects. It does not eat the old skin as geckos do. Moulting is controlled by thyroid hormones.

Dalmatian Wall Lizard
Podarcis melisellensis

Lacertidae

The Dalmatian Wall Lizard, with roughly 18 geographical subspecies, is another very variable lizard. It is distributed over the western part of the Balkan Peninsula and on numerous islands along the coast of Yugoslavia, where it lives on stony slopes and cliffs exposed to the full glare of the sun. Here and there it ascends to altitudes of 1,200 metres, but more often it is to be seen on the seashore, running nimbly over the rocks.

The sexes are easily distinguished by their colouring. The males usually have a green back patterned with rows of spots arranged in stripes, and on their sides they have rows of larger brown spots. The females may be a similar colour to the males, but without any spots, or they may be brown, with light longitudinal stripes. The belly of sexually adult males may change colour from pale yellow to deep yellow and bright orange.

The Milos Wall Lizard, *Podarcis milensis,* inhabits the Cyclades and islands in the vicinity of Milos, where it forms three subspecies. The most widely distributed is *P. m. milensis. P. m. schweizeri* occurs only on the island of Eremomilos and *P. m. gerakuniae* lives only on Gerakunia. It occurs in the same ecosystems as the preceding species and similarly feeds mainly on small insects.

The Dalmatian Wall Lizard (1) attains a total length of 16 – 18 cm. The Milos Wall Lizard (2) is slightly smaller. Male Milos Wall Lizards have a noticeably dark head and sides, while the females are lighter and have prominent light stripes. Erhard's Wall Lizard, *Podarcis erhardii* (3), is closely related to both the above species.

The general anatomy (4) of all lizards is the same. The heart is divided into two

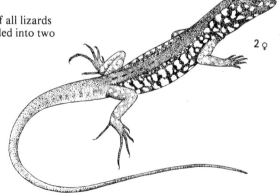

2 ♀

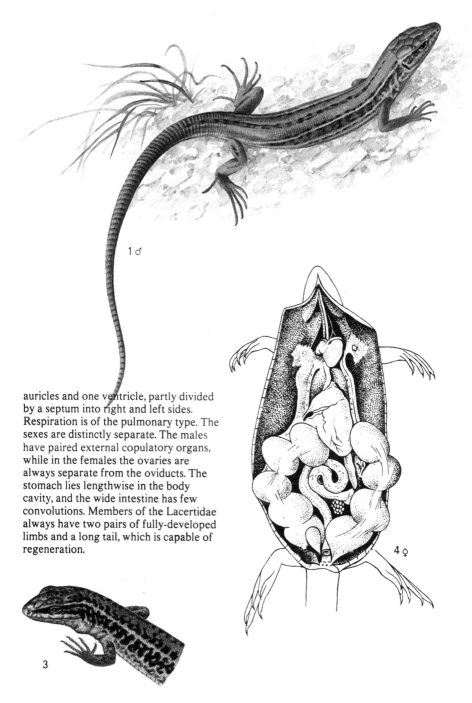

auricles and one ventricle, partly divided
by a septum into right and left sides.
Respiration is of the pulmonary type. The
sexes are distinctly separate. The males
have paired external copulatory organs,
while in the females the ovaries are
always separate from the oviducts. The
stomach lies lengthwise in the body
cavity, and the wide intestine has few
convolutions. Members of the Lacertidae
always have two pairs of fully-developed
limbs and a long tail, which is capable of
regeneration.

1 ♂

3

4 ♀

Balkan Wall Lizard
Podarcis taurica
Lacertidae

The area of distribution of the Balkan Wall Lizard stretches from the islands in the Aegean, across the south-eastern part of the Balkan Peninsula, to the Crimea. It is the most common reptile on the Bulgarian shore of the Black Sea. It has no particular requirements as regards its habitat and lives virtually anywhere — in roadside ditches, on shrub-covered hillsides, in pastureland and in deciduous woods. In the latter it grows to a considerable size and is almost as large as the Sand Lizard. The back of the males of Black Sea populations is not very distinctively coloured.

Isolated populations between the Danube and the river Tisa are always found on sandy soil — on river banks, on the remains of sand tips and often in the middle of swamps. The lizards here are smaller and slimmer (rather like the Wall Lizard) and the males have a luminous, bright green back. They dart like lightning among the clumps of vegetation in the sand and hide in holes no deeper than 50 cm. Once in their burrow they generally stay a few centimetres from the opening.

In the Crimea the Balkan Wall Lizard lives on the coast and on mountain steppes. If the summer is particularly hot it aestivates, while if the winter is mild it does not hibernate.

The female lays 2—6 eggs (usually 3) in May or June and the minute young hatch towards the end of the summer.

The habits, diet and hibernation period of the Balkan Wall Lizard are similar to those of the Sand Lizard.

Four subspecies of the Balkan Wall Lizard have been described. *Podarcis taurica taurica* (1) inhabits a substantial part of the total area of distribution, *P. t. ionica* lives in Greece and Albania and *P. t. gaigeae* and *P. t. thasopulae* occur on islands in the Aegean Sea.

2 ♂

142

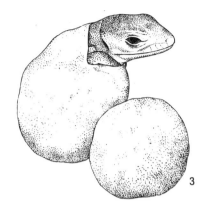

The splendidly coloured Peloponnese Wall Lizard *P. peloponnesiaca* (2), is to be found only on the Peloponnese Peninsula, where it frequents sunny rocks, olive groves and the walls of both historic ruins and ordinary houses. The males have turquoise markings on their sides, the females gold, gleaming stripes down their backs. This lizard lives at all altitudes on the peninsula, from sea level to high up in the mountains.

Inside the egg the little lizard is curled up into a tight ball. Prior to hatching, the parchment-like shell is saturated and softened by a fluid from within. The young lizard tears a hole in the shell with its snout, pokes its head out and then wriggles the rest of its body through. Its head is remarkably large in relation to the size of the egg (3).

3

1 ♂

143

Bedriaga's Rock Lizard
Lacerta bedriagae
Lacertidae

Bedriaga's Rock Lizard is the Mediterranean counterpart of the Viviparous Lizard. It has been found only on Corsica, where the nominate subspecies lives, and on Sardinia, where the subspecies *L. b. pressleri* and *L. b. sardoa* occur.

It is encountered primarily at high altitudes, from 600 to over 2,000 metres and descends to the coast only in the north of Sardinia. Woods with streams and pools provide its characteristic habitat, and these lizards are to be found right by the water's edge, or lying on stones projecting above the water. They often enter the water itself and are skilled swimmers. As distinct from older animals, the young have a bright green-blue tail, which in adults is 1.5 times the length of the body. Adult specimens have a total length of 20 cm. The Tyrrhenian Wall Lizard, *Podarcis tiliguerta,* also inhabits Corsica, Sardinia and smaller neighbouring islands, but it lives in quite different surroundings from the preceding species. It also occurs at high altitudes, but is to be encountered chiefly in hilly country, in dry, sunny, rocky places. It also frequents dry hillsides and roadside ditches. Of the two subspecies, *P. t. toro* lives only on the tiny island of Toro to the southwest of Sardinia. Both subspecies measure 25 cm, which is divided equally between their body and their tail.

Both Bedriaga's Rock Lizard and the Tyrrhenian Wall Lizard feed mainly on insects.

2 ♂

3 ♀

Adult male specimens of Bedriaga's Rock Lizard (1) attain a total length of up to 28 cm.

The males of the Tyrrhenian Wall Lizard (2) are generally more gaudily marked than the females (3), which always have light longitudinal stripes on a brown backround.

Members of the Lacertidae have undifferentiated teeth attached to the inner margin of the jawbones (4). When old teeth drop out, new ones grow in their place.

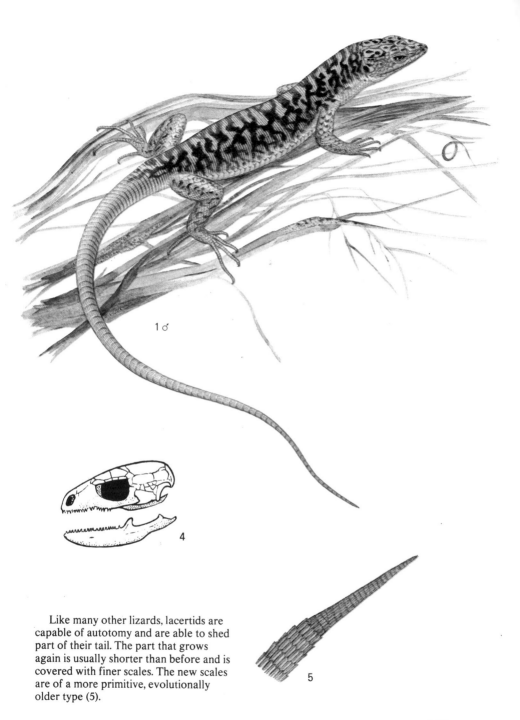

1 ♂

4

Like many other lizards, lacertids are capable of autotomy and are able to shed part of their tail. The part that grows again is usually shorter than before and is covered with finer scales. The new scales are of a more primitive, evolutionally older type (5).

5

Sharp-snouted Rock Lizard
Lacerta oxycephala   Lacertidae

This is a flat-bodied lizard with a long, flat head. Its tail is double
the length of its body and its total length can amount to 20 cm. In
addition to typically coloured individuals with reticular markings,
completely black specimens with a cobalt blue throat are occasionally encountered, mainly in places at a high altitude or in island
populations.

The Sharp-snouted Rock Lizard climbs better than any of the other
European lizards. It inhabits limestone mountains at altitudes up to
1,500 metres. Along the coasts and on islands it frequents the walls of
old stone buildings with open crevices into which its flat body allows
it to slip well out of reach of enemies. It climbs the highest walls and
has been sighted as high as 30 metres above the ground. Tourists in
particular like to watch its antics on the walls of the medieval harbour
fortress of Korcula in Yugoslavia.

It is distributed over a small area of Dalmatia, Hercegovina and
Montenegro, including some of the off-shore islands. It is interesting
to note that the similar Mosor Rock Lizard, *Lacerta mosorensis,* occupies approximately the same area.

The female lays her eggs in early summer and the young hatch six
weeks later. They measure 5 cm, are very nimble and feed on small
insects.

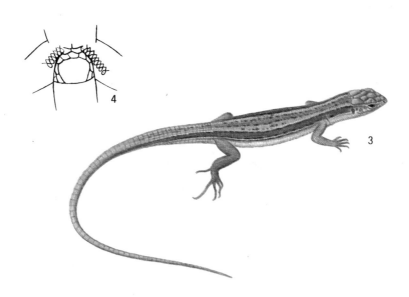

The markings on the body and tail of the Sharp-snouted Rock Lizard are very different (1).

The Mosor Rock Lizard, *Lacerta mosorensis* (2), occupies roughly the same area as the Sharp-snouted Rock Lizard. It lives mostly at altitudes of 600 — 1,500 metres and is common in the massif above Kotor Bay in Yugoslavia, for instance. The many shady spots in the rough-hewn limestone mountains, with their deep fissures, recesses and caves, are exactly what the lizard needs, although its actual incidence is determined by the high rainfall in these places.

The Meadow Lizard, *Lacerta praticola* (3), which inhabits a few small isolated areas in the north-east of the Balkan Peninsula and in the Caucasus, resembles the Viviparous Lizard and the two are often confused. Their main difference is

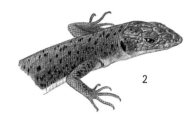

their anal plate, which in the Meadow Lizard is larger and ringed by only a single row of small scales (4), while in the Viviparous Lizard it is small and is surrounded by several rings of small scales. The Meadow Lizard inhabits stream banks, meadows round mountain springs and other moist areas where there is lush vegetation.

Iberian Rock Lizard
Lacerta monticola
Lacertidae

This lizard, which measures 16—20 cm, is to be encountered only in high mountains on the Iberian Peninsula, where it forms four subspecies. *L. m. monticola* lives in the Serra da Estrèla in Portugal, *L. m. bonnali* in the Bigorre region, in the French Pyrenees and *L. m. cyreni* in the Sierra de Guadarrama and the Sierra de Gredos in Spain, while *L. m. cantabrica* took its name from the Cantabrian Mountains in north-west Spain, where it was first discovered. These very hardy lizards are also generally active in the winter, and on sunny days can even be seen running about on the snow. They often frequent the outskirts of woods, or live in clumps of pines or juniper bushes. In their localities they usually form small communities. They are excellent climbers.

The incidence of the Maltese Wall Lizard, *Podarcis filfolensis*, is confined to a few islands — Malta, Gozo, Linosa and some of the Pelagian Islands. It takes its specific name from one of its localities, Filfola Rock. It measures about 15 cm. It is able to survive in the most inhospitable places, such as bare rocks jutting up out of the sea, but it also lives in gardens, in dry meadows and on stony roadsides.

Small species of lizards, like the Maltese Wall Lizard itself, often colonize areas where other wingless vertebrates would fail to find any sustenance for even a short time. The lizards not only live there permanently, however, but also breed there. On the bare rocks they feed on small insects and during inclement weather they retire into deep clefts and holes in the rocks. Here the females also lay their eggs.

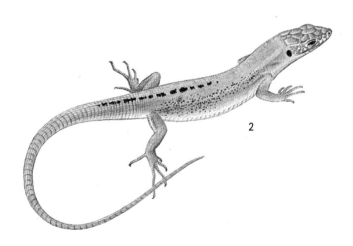

2

The male Iberian Rock Lizard (1) is found in a variety of colours. Specimens from some localities have a green, black-spotted back and bluish sides. Sexually adult males also have a variably coloured belly, from light green to pink or bright orange. The females are an inconspicuous shade of brown, with traces of dark stripes down their back.

The Maltese Wall Lizard (2) is also very variably coloured, and in addition to spotted forms almost unicoloured grey-green individuals are often found. The males also have more distinctive markings.

1

Greek Rock Lizard
Lacerta graeca   Lacertidae

Like the Peloponnese Wall Lizard, this species is also confined to the Peloponnese Peninsula in the southern part of Greece. It is a moderately large, flat-backed lizard with a pointed snout. Its tail is two and a half times the length of its body (which measures 8 cm). This indicates that the animal is a very good climber.

It is less abundant than the Peloponnese Wall Lizard, and its localities lie above 400 metres. It frequents places near water, where the vegetation provides shade. It is to be found on walls, vineyard terraces and roadsides, in ditches and on rock faces with shady fissures. If the sun is too hot, it shelters in the shade of tall vegetation and it even lives in open woods.

The markings of the Green Rock Lizard are not very varied and the only differences are in the size of the spots. Its neck, belly, the first third of its tail and the inner surface of its limbs are a vivid yellow with small dark spots.

Its diet consists mainly of insects and other arthropods. It catches its food in the same way as most other lizards, approaching very cautiously to within a short distance of its prey and then pouncing on it. If several lizards attack the same large victim at once, they fight over it until it is torn to pieces and eaten.

2

1 ♂

The Greek Rock Lizard is really
a mountain-dweller. The males (1) are
more densely spotted than the females,
but otherwise the two sexes have almost
the same appearance.

Horvath's Rock Lizard, *Lacerta
horvathi,* inhabits the mountains of
north-western Yugoslavia and the
adjoining part of Italy (2). It is smaller
than the other two, has plainer markings
and is somewhat reminiscent of the
nominate form of the Wall Lizard.

151

Slow-worm
Anguis fragilis
Anguidae

Although the Slow-worm is a lizard, a lay observer might easily mistake it for a snake. This is probably the reason why so many of these harmless animals suffer an untimely death.

The species is distributed over practically the whole of Europe except Ireland and northern Scandinavia. It also inhabits north-west Afrika, Asia Minor, the north-western part of Iran, Transcaucasia and western Siberia. In most parts of its territory it occurs from the lowlands to above the forest limit in the mountains. It can be encountered on the outskirts of woods and thickets, in wooded steppes and in cultivated country, in gardens and on banks overgrown with bushes. The only places it shuns are wet meadows and peat-bogs.

Since slow-worms themselves are usually slow-moving, they have to catch slow-moving prey, such as worms and slugs. They are most active after dusk and spend the day in hiding or basking in mild sunshine. Very often they shelter in rotting tree stumps, in piles of stones or among decaying leaves. After rain they come out of hiding, because this is when they are most likely to find worms and slugs.

Slow-worms are ovoviviparous. The young are born at the end of August or the beginning of September. They usually number 5—26 and measure about 10 cm. They have the same diet as adult slow-worms and become sexually mature after three years. The Slow-worm is long-lived and has been known to survive for 54 years in captivity.

The Slow-worm is either solitary or forms pairs. The duration of hibernation depends on the climate, beginning in October and usually ending in March or April, or in its most northerly haunts, not until the first half of May. Slow-worms generally hibernate in the roots of trees, at a depth of about 70 cm, often in groups of several dozen.

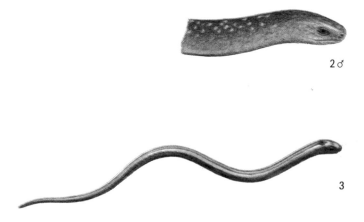

2 ♂

3

Slow-worms can attain a length of 50 cm, about 30 cm of which is the tail, the males being usually slimmer and longer than the females. The three known subspecies are differentiated by the arrangement of the scales on their head, the shape of their body and their different colouring. The area of the nominate subspecies, *Anguis fragilis fragilis* (1), stretches from Africa to the Carpathian Mountains. Further east comes *A. f. colchicus*, often with blue spots, which are more pronounced in the

older males (2). *A. f. peloponnesiacus* has so far been found only on the Peloponnese peninsula.

As distinct from the adult animals, the young (3) are a bright coppery brown colour, with one or two fine dark stripes down their back.

Slow-worms are famous for their fragile tail (hence the name of the species) and old individuals generally have a regenerated tail, which has often been replaced several times.

European Glass Lizard
Ophisaurus apodus

Anguidae

The European Glass Lizard resembles a snake in size and appearance, but its eyelids, open auditory orifices and other characters show it to be a lizard and closely related to the Slow-worm. It inhabits only the warmer countries of Europe, the Balkan Peninsula, the southern coast of the Crimea, the Black Sea coast of the Caucasus and Transcaucasia, continuing from there into central Asia.

It is a large reptile up to 130 cm in length and it is most likely to be found basking in the sun on the outskirts of a vineyard, in an open wood or in an olive grove. In central Asia it also lives on rounded hills covered only with loess and short grass, where it shelters in rodent burrows. It is a good swimmer and can stay for a long time in water.

When disturbed, it can move surprisingly quickly, though noisily. When hunting, however, it approaches its prey soundlessly. It can also climb high up into the tops of trees. It hibernates under the roots of trees and shrubs and reappears in March or April.

Its diet is very varied and comprises slugs, snails, worms, small rodents and young birds. It has a special predilection for lizards and snakes, venomous snakes included. It is said to have been introduced to tourist centres in the Mediterranean region, to combat the Nose-horned Viper.

Adult specimens are usually a uniform colour, from light yellow in the Caucasus and central Asia to coffee-coloured in the Mediterranean region. The tail is not easily detached and does not regenerate completely if lost.

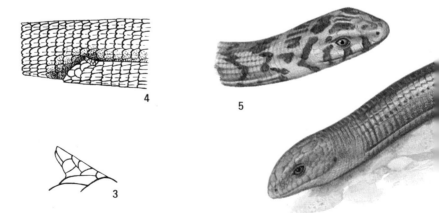

4

5

3

The European Glass Lizard (1) has a massive head, which in the males is noticeably wider than the body. Its teeth are short and blunt and at the back of its jaws there are a few stud-like teeth, used for crushing larger prey and snail shells. Its body is covered with tough scales, each of which consists of a bony plate (2) covered with a thin layer of keratin. Along its sides, running the whole length of its body, is a respiratory groove — a loose fold of skin covered with small, soft scales. On either side of the cloaca there is a small outgrowth, measuring 3—4 mm, the rudiment of the longest digit of the hind limb (3 — a detail, 4 — a general view of the cloacal region).

At the end of June or in July the European Glass Lizard lays 6—10 eggs. The newly-hatched young bear little resemblance to their parents (5), since they have vividly contrasting markings and the pronounced ridges on their scales form sharp, prominent rows all down their body.

2

1

155

Snake-eyed Skink
Ablepharus kitaibelii   Scincidae

The Snake-eyed Skink is a dainty little animal less than 10 cm long. It belongs to the family Scincidae, which is distributed mainly over the tropical and subtropical belt in every continent. The area of distribution of the Snake-eyed Skink is centred in Asia Minor and the south-eastern part of the Balkan Peninsula, while its marginal, north-western populations inhabit scattered, disconnected enclaves.

In Europe, the Snake-eyed Skink extends further north than any other member of the family. It lives mostly in fallen leaves on the outskirts of warm oak woods, or on wooded steppes where downy oaks and other deciduous trees grow. The best way to find it is to listen to the sounds it makes among dry fallen leaves, where it catches spiders and small insects. It is diurnal. Sexual dimorphism is not very pronounced and the only obvious difference is that the males have longer limbs than the females. The female lays 2—4 leathery-shelled eggs about 5 mm long, in a hole in the ground. Snake-eyed skinks usually hibernate from October to April, but the actual time depends on the climate.

The Snake-eyed Skink is very timid, and when disturbed, it hides under the nearest stone or among dry leaves. For fast movement it holds its limbs close to its body and glides along like a snake. It is intolerant of members of its own species and the males in particular fight mercilessly with each other.

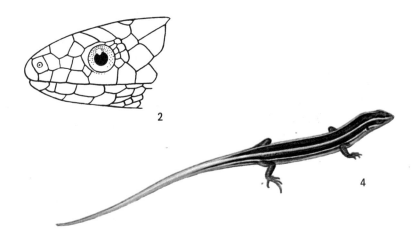

2

4

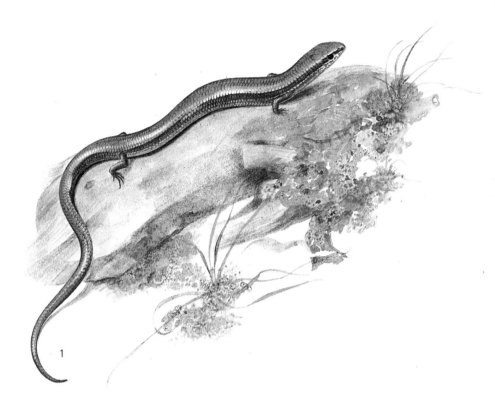

3

Five subspecies of this tiny skink have been described. *Ablepharus kitaibelii kitaibelii* lives in Greece and Asia Minor, *A. k. fitzingeri* (1) in central Europe, *A. k. stepaneki* in Rumania, *A. k. fabichi* on the islands in the Aegean and *A. k. chernovi* in Armenia and Turkey.

One of the most important characters of the genus *Ablepharus* are the fused and completely transparent eyelids so that the eyes resemble those of a snake (2).

The smooth, hard body of skinks (Scincidae) is due to their scales, which are firmly fixed in the corium. In addition, each of the scales is supported by a hard underlying bony platelet (3) with an interwoven network of fine canals. Some skinks, like the young of the Common Western Skink, *Eumeces skiltonianus,* of North America (4), have a handsome metallic sheen.

Ocellated Skink
Chalcides ocellatus

Scincidae

The Ocellated Skink, which lives in northern Africa, southern Europe and western Asia, is a common representative of the skink family. Although it can attain a total length of 30 cm, it is usually shorter, and European specimens generally measure about 20 cm.

Ocellated skinks inhabit very dry lowland localities with sandy or loamy ground. They are diurnal and often occur in one place in large numbers. They hide under stones or in burrows, or cleverly wriggle out of sight into loose topsoil. They require heat and often warm themselves on hot stones. They live mainly on insects and other invertebrates, but large specimens occasionally attack small lizards.

The females give birth to 6—15 live young — large females producing even more. Newborn skinks measure about 6 cm and feed on small insects. The young are very active and can burrow quickly in sand the first day after they are born.

Four subspecies of the Ocellated Skink occur in Europe. *Chalcides ocellatus ocellatus* also lives in north-western Africa and western Asia, *C. o. linosae* lives only on the island of Linosa, the area of *C. o. tiligugu* stretches from north-western Africa to the islands of Sardinia, Malta, Sicily and Pantelleria and *C. o. zavattarii* occurs mainly on Lampedusa and the Isola del Conigli. Ocellated skinks are very variably marked, but are basically a light olive shade with dark spots.

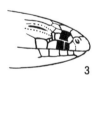

3

4

The wedge-shaped snout, smooth, overlapping scales and cylindrical body of the Ocellated Skink (1) enable it to burrow in the ground. The males have a larger head than the smaller-bodied females, but otherwise there are no outward differences between the sexes.

Bedriaga's Skink, *Chalcides bedriagai* (2), is a species inhabiting the Iberian Peninsula. It has a maximum length of 16 cm, half of which is accounted for by the tail. This skink also lives in low-lying country, on sandy ground with sparse vegetation. If in danger, it hides under the stones on which it basks, or burrows in the sand. The females give birth to only two or three live young.

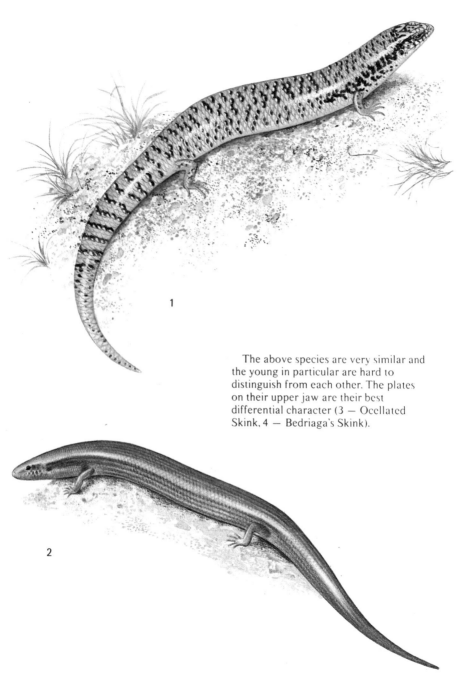

1

The above species are very similar and the young in particular are hard to distinguish from each other. The plates on their upper jaw are their best differential character (3 — Ocellated Skink, 4 — Bedriaga's Skink).

2

Three-toed Skink
Chalcides chalcides

Scincidae

A glance at this skink in its natural surroundings might give the impression that this is a snake or at least a slow-worm. The Three-toed Skink does not use its very rudimentary limbs for locomotion at all, but glides along like a snake or a slow-worm. If disturbed, it disappears extraordinarily quickly and can be described in general as very nimble.

Unlike other European skinks, it does not frequent dry places. On the contrary, during both drought and cold weather it retires to deep underground shelters beneath the roots of trees or under stones. It occurs most frequently in lowlands, in localities with lush green vegetation, and it also lives in damp meadows. It feeds mainly on invertebrates and its agility enables it to catch insects on the wing. It is diurnal. The female gives birth to 15—23 live young.

The Three-toed Skink inhabits south-western Europe and the part of Africa facing it. Four subspecies are known in Europe — *C. c. chalcides* in Italy, Sicily and Elba, *C. c. concolor* in the neighbourhood of Rome, *C. c. striatus* in the south of France and the Iberian Peninsula and *C. c. vittatus* on Sardinia.

C. moseri is another member of the genus living in Europe, but it is exceedingly rare and it is even uncertain whether it still exists. It occurs only on the Greek island of Santorin, where it was discovered in 1937, but has not been found since. It has only two toes on its forelimbs, but four on its hind limbs.

The Three-toed Skink (1) measures up to 42 cm, including its tail.

The Greek Legless Skink, *Ophiomorus punctatissimus* (2), a species living in the south of Greece, on the island of Kithira and in south-western Asia, looks like a slow-worm and is likewise limbless. It grows to a length of 20 cm, inhabits grassy localities and feeds on insects. If in danger, it tries to divert the attention of its attacker to its tail, which is more strikingly coloured than its small head. Nine species of the genus *Ophiomorus* are known in all.

Schneider's Skink, *Eumeces schneideri*, lives in Transcaucasia in eastern Europe,

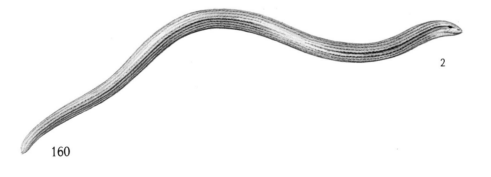

2

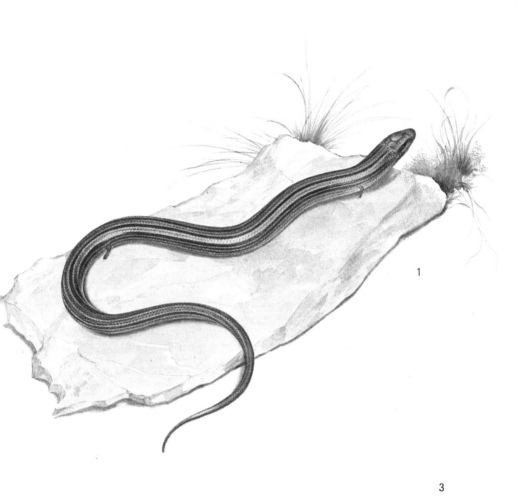

1

and several subspecies occur in northern
Africa and southern Asia, including India.
The various subspecies are differently
coloured and of different sizes. They all
feed mainly on insects and the females
lay 6—9 eggs. Fig. 3 shows the European
distribution of members of the genus
Chalcides.

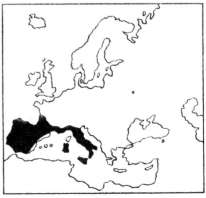

Grey Amphisbaena
Blanus cinereus

Amphisbaenidae

This sole European member of the family Amphisbaenidae is an interesting reptile inhabiting pinewoods and cultivated land in the southernmost two thirds of the Iberian Peninsula. It can attain a length of 30 cm and is very variably coloured. Individual scales cannot be detected on the surface of its body as in other reptiles, since it is covered with skin cross-grooved to produce an effect of annular segments like those of annelid worms. Fine longitudinal grooves give the impression that the body is covered with small squares. The skin is loose, and the reptile makes use of this for locomotion, moving like an earthworm. It can also glide like a snake.

The front of its massive head is covered with a large plate enabling it to burrow more easily. Its eyes, which are covered with a skin, are visible only as dark spots. They are evidently able to register only light and dark, or at most to distinguish vague outlines. Although its sight is so imperfect, its sense of smell, touch and taste are very well developed.

The Grey Amphisbaena is generally to be found below the surface of the soil, under a stone or in an anthill. Ants and other arthropods found in the soil are the chief components of its diet. It seldom appears in the open except occasionally after heavy rain. If in danger, it tucks its head under its coiled body and waves its short, massive tail in the face of its enemy. Owing to its secret way of life no reliable information on how it reproduces is available.

2

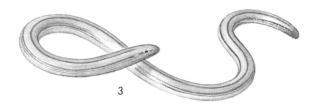

Amphisbaenians look very like earthworms. They have a blunt-tipped head and tail and a segmented instead of a scaly body. Their tiny eyes are lidless. Some species possess forelimbs, while others are limbless. They live in soil and their diet consists mainly of ants and termites.

The Grey Amphisbaena (1) is one of 130 members of this curious family. It lives in northern Africa as well as in Europe.

The Worm Lizard, *Rhineura floridana* (2), is the only representative of this family in the United States. On its tail it has large, rough scales, which it uses to support itself on the walls of its burrows. The family Anniellidae is endemic to the south-western part of the United States. The only two known species resemble worm lizards, but have well-developed eyes with movable lids (3 — the Footless Lizard, *Anniella pulchra,* of California).

163

Worm Snake
Typhlops vermicularis   Typhlopidae

The Worm Snake is one of the most curious members of this order. It is only likely to be encountered by an extremely lucky chance, or after a long, hard search, though it is by no means rare in its native territory.

In Europe it lives in the southern part of the Balkan Peninsula, and on the Greek islands. In Africa it is found mainly in northern Egypt, and in Asia it occurs beyond the mountains of the Caucasus. It spends the greater part of the day hidden away under stones or (more often) in deep underground burrows which it excavates itself.

In south-eastern Europe it is seen in the most diverse habitats and is to be found in moist localities in the mountains, on sandy shores and in dry steppe country.

Worm snakes do not display sexual dimorphism. In May and June the females lay 6—8 elongate eggs measuring about 11 mm, which they hide in burrows specially dug in the ground.

The Worm Snake is a representative of a uniform, phylogenetically very primitive family numbering over 200 species inhabiting warm regions throughout the world. All have rudimentary eyes capable only of distinguishing between darkness and light. They have a small, tight mouth and thick, exceptionally smooth skin covered with tiny scales that shine like glass. Since they feed almost entirely on ant pupae, they need a thick body covering to protect them from ant bites. Very often they can be caught in quite large numbers near or inside anthills. All worm snakes have minute teeth in their upper jaw only.

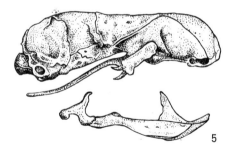

5

At first sight, the Worm Snake, *Typhlops vermicularis,* (1) looks like a glossy, brownish pink earthworm. It can be up to 35 cm long, but measures only 3—6 mm across. The tail is thicker than the tiny head and, apart from the concealed mode of life of the animal, is its only defence. Enemies are inclined to attack the tail rather than the head, which the snake in any case tries to tuck away out of sight.

164

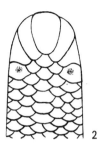  

2   3   4

The head is armed with wide, smooth horny plates (2 — from above, 3 — from below, 4 — in profile) which, together with the powerful skull (5), enable it to burrow in the ground.

Although actually harmless and helpless, the Worm Snake is often regarded by the ignorant as a dangerous, venomous animal.

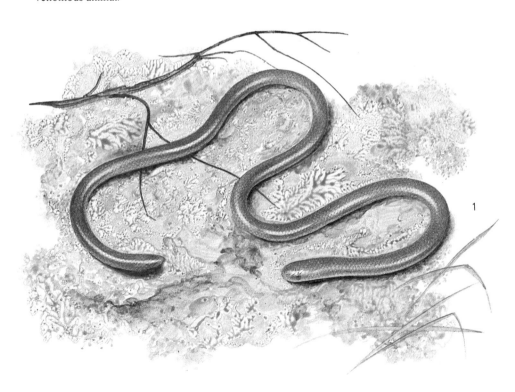

1

Sand Boa
Eryx jaculus
Boidae

Only one genus of boas (Boidae), the genus *Eryx*, lives in Europe. The majority of its 10 species, which inhabit Africa, Asia and Europe, are inconspicuously coloured (the brightly marked African Sand Boa, *E. colubrinus*, is an exception) and are adapted to a subterranean mode of life. Sand boas have a short, blunt tail, no distinct division between their head and body and very small eyes.

The Sand Boa, which attains a maximum length of 80 cm, bears little resemblance to its tropical cousins, the giant boas and pythons, which can grow to a length of 9 metres. It seeks out the warmest localities, such as bush-covered slopes in river valleys, on which large stones providing adequate shelter are scattered. It also occurs in open steppeland thinly overgrown with shrubs, where it shelters mainly in rodent burrows. It comes out after dusk and is only likely to be seen in the early morning, basking briefly in the sun.

These sand boas feed mainly on lizards and rodents (particularly the young). They wrap their strong body coils round their prey and suffocate it in exactly the same way as the big constricting snakes. At the end of August and the beginning of September the female gives birth to up to 20 young measuring about 14 cm. These feed chiefly on small lizards, which they are immediately able to suffocate.

Balkan populations belong to the subspecies *Eryx jaculus turcicus*. *E. jaculus familiaris* occurs in Transcaucasia.

One of the characteristics of boas and pythons is that they still possess rudimentary pelvic bones and hind limbs.

This peculiarity is common to all the members of the family Boidae and outwardly it takes the form of a small

2

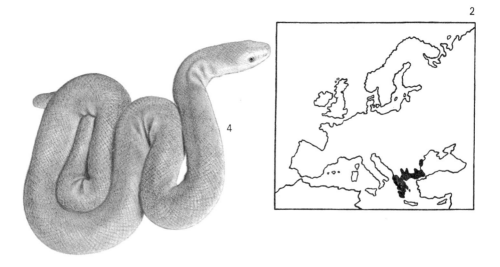

4

claw protruding between the scales on
either side of the cloaca (3).

Eryx jaculus turcicus (1) inhabits
northern Africa, south-western Asia and,
in Europe, the south-eastern part of the
Balkan Peninsula. Isolated finds have also
been reported in the Dobrogea region
(Rumania) (2). Another European species,
the Desert Sand Boa, *Eryx miliaris,* lives
in sandy regions by the Caspian Sea. It
differs from the others in length, and in
the position of its eyes. These are situated
on top of its head, while those of the
Sand Boa are situated on the sides of the
head.

The Rubber Boa, *Charina bottae* (4),
is a small snake found in the west of the
United States. When in danger it hides its
head in its coils and exposes its less
vulnerable tail to its enemy.

Montpellier Snake
Malpolon monspessulanus   Colubridae

The very agile Montpellier Snake, which is about 200 cm long, belongs to the group of poisonous colubrid snakes. In the back of its upper jaw it has enlarged, grooved teeth, each with a poison gland at its root, communicating with the groove. The venom is used to kill prey, mainly lizards, snakes and small rodents. Animals bitten by this snake die very quickly, and its bite can also have unpleasant consequences such as painful local swelling, possibly together with a bad headache, for humans.

The Montpellier snake frequents dry, stony localities inhabited by large numbers of lizards. In Macedonia it has been found in piles of stones around the edges of fields and near the ruins of old buildings. When hunting, it stops from time to time and rears the front of its body high above the ground, attentively turning its head at the same time, so that it somewhat resembles a cobra in its characteristic pose. If in danger it hisses loudly and attacks the intruder with its mouth closed.

In the second half of April the female lays up to 20 eggs. She usually deposits them in safe spaces in piles of stones so that they retain the moisture essential for the healthy development of the embryos. The young snakes feed on insects — mainly orthopterous insects and beetles.

The distribution area of the Montpellier Snake includes northern Africa, western Asia and southern Europe except Italy. This snake also lives in Transcaucasia and along the lower reaches of the river Volga. The Iberian Peninsula and north-western Africa are inhabited by the nominate subspecies *Malpolon monspessulanus monspessulanus,* and *M. m. insignitus* inhabits the remainder of the area.

3

2

The Montpellier Snake has one marked feature differentiating it from other European colúbrids. This is the sharp, prominent ridge above its eyes, which makes it look as though it is frowning (1). Its large eyes are evidence of good vision and, in fact, vision is its most important sense. As distinct from the adult snakes, the young have contrasting spots (2).

Ravergier's Whip Snake, *Coluber* *ravergieri nummifer* (3), which occurs very occasionally on the island of Rhodes, also has weak venom and grooved teeth. The nominate subspecies *C. r. ravergieri*, which lives in central Asia and the Caucasus, sometimes occurs in an interesting black-headed form (4). *C. r. chernovi*, another subspecies, lives in Transcaucasia, just beyond the borders of Europe.

4

1

Horseshoe Whip Snake
Coluber hippocrepis Colubridae

This robust and variably coloured snake attains a length of up to 200 cm. The species has only fairly recently been divided into two subspecies. Zoogeographically, *Coluber hippocrepis hippocrepis* is a typically Mediterranean element. It inhabits the south-eastern coast of the Iberian Peninsula, Sardinia, Malta and Sicily and extends to the northwestern coast of Africa, to Morocco, Algeria and Tunisia. *C. h. intermedius* (formerly included in the species *C. algirus* or *C. florulentus*) has been found only in Morocco and in a small adjacent part of Algeria, near the town of Ain-Sefra. The two subspecies differ chiefly as regards the number of dorsal scales per transverse row. Their other characters are not distinctly separate.

Throughout its area of distribution the Horseshoe Whip Snake frequents dry, stony localities covered with a thin sprinkling of shrubs. Although it is a good climber, like most of the members of this genus it lives on the ground. It is a diurnal snake. When not basking in the sun, in the morning or late afternoon, it generally hides under stones, in rodent burrows or in loose stone embankments bordering fields and vineyards. When disturbed, it usually makes a quick escape, but sometimes it offers determined resistance and tries intimidation by means of loud hissing.

In early spring the females lay 5—10 longish white eggs, which they hide in warm, sandy soil under stones. The young are born at the beginning of summer and at first they catch mainly lizards. The adults also devour small mammals and birds. Males and females are identical in appearance.

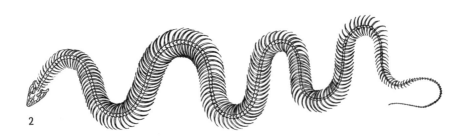

2

The Horseshoe Whip Snake (1) takes its name from the typical configuration of its markings, which form stripes in the shape of a horseshoe on the sides of its neck.

The simplicity and symmetry of the body of a snake is due to the structure of its skeleton (2), which is composed of a skull, a spine and ribs. A vestigial pelvis and the rudiments of limbs are present in only a few of the more primitive families. The skull is fragile and the powerful, flexibly connected jaws enable the snake to swallow bulky food. The ribs, which are sometimes already joined to the second vertebra, all have virtually the same structure and shape. They are extremely important, as in part they replace the missing limbs. The snake supports itself on the abdominal end of the ribs and uses them to propel itself forwards. The number of vertebrae is exceptionally high and varies from 200 to over 400.

1

Algerian Whip Snake
Coluber algirus   Colubridae

The stony terraces along hillside roads, piles of stones and bush-covered slopes where stones abound are the home of the Algerian Whip Snake, a warmth-loving emissary from the African ophidian fauna to Europe. It is common in north-western Africa, but in Europe it occurs only on Malta and even there it is very rare.

It has a slender, but firm body and its movements resemble the twists and turns of a springy wire. It seldom measures more than 100 cm. Its small, sharp-tipped head is notable for the large eyes, which have round pupils. Since it is diurnal, its good vision plays an important role in the search for food. The snake raises the front of its body and surveys its surroundings, looking for lizards and small rodents. When it sights prey it approaches slowly and carefully, but if the victim runs away, the snake is usually able to catch up with it, even if it is a large, agile lizard. It chases prey over only short distances, however, and if the other animal has a chance of escaping, the snake is very soon aware of this and gives up the chase. When it succeeds in catching an animal, it grips it firmly in its jaws, using its body to hold the other in place. It does not coil itself tightly round the victim, like members of the genus *Elaphe,* but in loose coils, simply keeping the animal pressed to the ground to prevent it from jerking itself free from the clutch of the small-toothed jaws.

2

The Algerian Whip Snake (1) has a slender body, admirably adapted for fast movement over uneven ground. The dark bars on its back (2) play an important role in passive defence. The undulating movements of its body produce a stroboscopic effect through oscillation of the stripes in the field of vision of the attacker, and that is often sufficient to scare it away.

Two interesting small snakes — *Eirenis collaris* and *Eirenis modestus* — are to be found in the Caucasus and on the shores of the Caspian Sea. They are not more than 50 cm long, live hidden away under stones and subsist on insects and other invertebrates. A European snake which lives mainly on insects is a rarity. In many cases the young eat them, but change in adulthood to other sources of food. Orsini's vipers and Caucasian vipers, whose diet still consists predominantly of insects in adulthood, are an exception.

1

Dahl's Whip Snake
Coluber najadum
Colubridae

Dahl's Whip Snake is a thin-bodied snake usually measuring no more than 80 cm, although exceptionally it can attain 130 cm. Its body proportions and behaviour are reminiscent of the tropical green whip snakes of the genus *Ahaetulla*. It inhabits stony, sunny slopes on foothills and mountains with evergreen vegetation or with tall grass. It can be seen only during the daytime, since at night it hides under stones and in clefts in the rocks. It hibernates in deep crevices.

Its area includes the Yugoslavian shores of the Adriatic, the Balkan countries, the Caucasus and western and central Asia. In the mountains it ascends to altitudes of 1,600—1,700 metres.

It is very fast-moving — indeed it is often difficult to follow it with the human eye. The best time to find it is between March and mid-September — preferably by looking under stones in the places where it occurs. It is only by chance that it can be seen in motion, as it streaks up into the security of the top of a bush. Once in safety, it may poke its head out for an instant to survey the intruder, but immediately afterwards it disappears again, usually for good. The lightness, swiftness and complete silence of its movements make the observer wonder if it was really a snake that he saw, or whether it was an optical illusion.

The large eyes testify to the excellent vision of this snake. Its diet consists mainly of various lizards, small rodents and insects (chiefly Orthoptera). At the end of June or in July, the female lays 3—5 (though sometimes up to 12) markedly elongate eggs in holes in the ground. The thin-bodied young, which measure up to 29 cm when hatched, live on insects and young lizards.

Balkan populations belong to the subspecies *Coluber najadum dahli* (1). The nominate subspecies, *C. n. najadum* (2), has been found in the Caucasus and in central Asia, Iran and Iraq. It has more spots on the front half of its body than the other subspecies and sometimes they

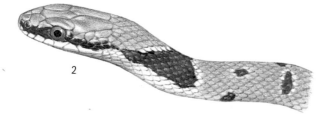

2

174

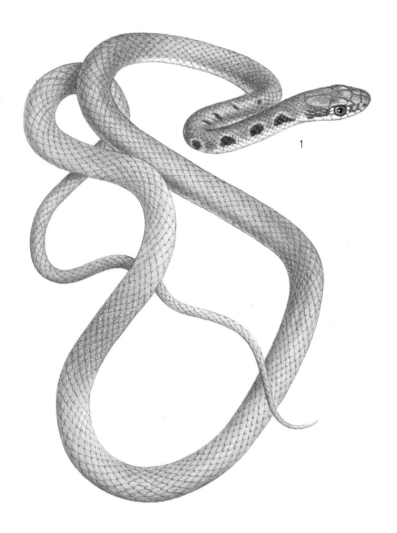

1

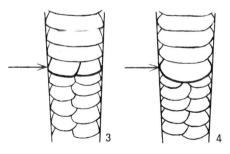

3

4

continue right down its body as far as the tail. The spots on the sides often merge to form a transverse stripe across the back. Plain glossy black specimens with a greyish-white belly are sometimes seen in mountain forests in the Caucasus.

The preanal scale is a useful character for a preliminary identification of an unknown snake in Europe. In all colubrid snakes it is divided (3), while in all vipers it is undivided (4).

175

Western Whip Snake
Coluber viridiflavus
Colubridae

The Western Whip Snake, which inhabits the western and central part of southern Europe, attains a length of up to 180 cm. The nominate subspecies, *Coluber viridiflavus viridiflavus*, inhabits north-western Spain, central and southern France, the south of Switzerland, north-western and central Italy and Sardinia, Corsica and Elba. The Black Whip Snake, *C. v. carbonarius*, lives in the southern foothills of the Alps, north-western Yugoslavia and north-eastern and southern Italy and on Sicily, Malta and the island of Pelagos.

The Western Whip Snake has a very varied diet, for in addition to various small mammals and birds, including their young, it devours lizards, blindworms, snakes, frogs and tadpoles, beetles and slugs and snails. When first hatched, the young live on small invertebrate animals.

This species is to be encountered in low-lying country and occurs chiefly in dry localities with only a thin sprinkling of shrubs. Like other colubrid snakes it moves very quickly, but if threatened it puts up a fight. To the accompaniment of loud hissing it sometimes attacks the enemy directly and if picked up it immediately tries to bite. It is a diurnal snake and often basks in the sun. At night it hides under stones or in the burrows of small mammals and in chilly weather it stays there all day. The females lay 8—15 white eggs measuring about 40 × 20 mm. The young, which hatch 6—8 weeks later, measure 25 cm.

This snake hibernates in a deep hole in the ground or below the roots of a bush.

2

On its back, *Coluber viridiflavus* has smooth scales arranged in 19 longitudinal rows. The ground colour of the nominate subspecies, *Coluber viridiflavus viridiflavus* (1), is black with greenish-yellow markings, while most specimens of the subspecies *C. v. carbonarius* (2) are a deep glossy black. The belly is always yellowish-brown.

As a rule, members of the genus *Coluber* do not kill their prey beforehand, but swallow it alive. Their fasten their teeth into large animals and maintain a hold on them by means of a few simple coils of their body (3), but the coils are not very tight and are often not strong

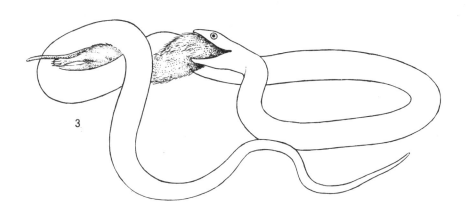

enough to kill the animal. Toxin has been found in some representatives of the genus. It is not injected into the prey by venom fangs, however, but simply trickles down the unmodified teeth.

3

1

Balkan Whip Snake
Coluber gemonensis   Colubridae

The Balkan Whip Snake frequents dry stony localities, vineyard terraces, olive groves and areas of evergreen scrub. It likes to lie in the sun near low, spreading shrubs, in which it seeks shelter if danger threatens. It is a typical terrestrial snake and does not care for climbing trees and bushes. Its average length is 100 cm, but occasionally it may measure up to 120 cm. Adult specimens are simply, but very elegantly coloured, with interesting markings which change almost imperceptibly from one type to another. The front of the body is spotted, while the middle is a plain grey or yellowish colour.

Lizards are the main prey of the Balkan Whip Snake, but it also hunts young birds and small mammals. The snake itself often falls prey to the European Glass Lizard.

The Balkan Whip Snake glides along very quickly, with its body outstretched, and seemingly without any undulations. If cornered, it defends itself bravely. Hissing loudly it coils its body into loose loops and strikes at its enemy from a considerable distance.

It is interesting to compare the area of distribution of this species with that of the Large Whip Snake, *Coluber jugularis.* On the Balkan Peninsula, wherever the Large Whip Snake is missing, its place is taken, as it were, by the Balkan Whip Snake. There is only one tiny part of the Albanian coast where the two areas overlap. The Balkan Whip Snake also inhabits a relatively small strip of the coast of Yugoslavia, Albania and southern Greece, including some of the islands.

The Balkan Whip Snake (1 — young specimen) is one of the 25 species of the genus *Coluber,* which inhabit Europe, practically the whole of Asia and North and Central America. One thing they all have in common, wherever they live, is that they are very spirited and, if in danger, will even make a stand against human beings. The Blue Racer, *Coluber constrictor* (2), is a common species in the United States. It likes to bask in the sun on top of a bush and has an extremely varied diet.

2

178

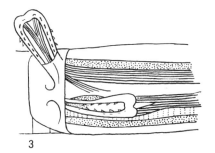

Male snakes have paired copulatory organs known as hemipenes, which, prior to copulation, can be thrust out on either side of the cloaca (3). When at rest they lie in capsules at the base of the tail, facing the tip. There are various outgrowths on the body of each hemipenis, some of them actually shaped like barbs.

3

1

Large Whip Snake
Coluber jugularis   Colubridae

With a length of almost 300 cm, the Large Whip Snake is the longest snake in Europe. It inhabits the Balkan Peninsula, except the Dalmatian coast, is abundant in the Black Sea region, extends to the Caucasus and also lives in western Asia. There is also evidence of an earlier occurrence in Czechoslovakia. The finds date from 1888 to 1922, but since then none have been reported. Reliable contemporary reports of its most northerly incidence come from the Mecsek, Vilanyi and Budaörs mountains near Budapest in Hungary. The Large Whip Snake ascends to an altitude of 1,500 metres.

In Bulgaria it is to be found chiefly on open pasture, where it frequents groups of trees and bushes. It has a thick, muscular body, is extremely agile and wary and a skilful climber, and if in direct danger it makes a brave stand. Before attacking it coils itself into a spiral, to the accompaniment of loud hissing, then strikes with an open mouth and attemps to bite. Its bite is not dangerous, but is very unpleasant, since it is impossible to free oneself immediately from the recurved teeth. It is claimed that it also attacks grazing cattle, biting them in the mouth, and in encounters with humans it evidently often considers attack to be the best form of defence.

Being so large, this snake eats bulky food and its normal diet comprises small mammals, birds, lizards and even snakes. It also catches large insects and occasionally devours amphibians.

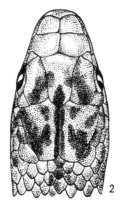

2

180

The European section of its area of distribution, together with northern Turkey, are inhabited by the subspecies *Coluber jugularis caspius* (1). The nominate subspecies, *C. j. jugularis,* lives in Turkey, Syria and Israel. The ground colour of *C. j. schmidti,* which lives in Transcaucasia and central Asia, is often red, and the top of its head is conspicuously spotted (2). The Asian Whip Snake, *C. j. asianus,* is known only in north-eastern Syria and Iraq.

In June and July the female lays 6—18 eggs about 50 mm long. The young, measuring about 28 cm, hatch at the beginning of September. They are spotted, bear little resemblance to their parents and have remarkably large eyes (3). They feed on insects and young lizards.

Leopard Snake
Elaphe situla   Colubridae

This most handsomely coloured European snake is now, unfortunately, very rare. It may well have been its gay red colour and markings that were responsible, as this snake is very conspicuous. Its maximum length is just under 100 cm.

It has a large area of distribution, but nowhere is it abundant. It is known to occur in southern Italy and Sicily, on the Yugoslavian coast of the Adriatic, in Albania and Greece, on some of the islands in the Aegean and in Asia Minor. It makes an occasional appearance in the Crimea, but a previous incidence in the Caucasus has not been confirmed for many years.

The Leopard Snake is a placid animal with a flexible body. It devours small rodents, young birds in the nest, and lizards. Like all members of the genus *Elaphe,* it kills its prey by suffocating it with its coils. When it is disturbed the tip of its tail vibrates and the sound it makes as it strikes the ground or rustles in the dry leaves is reminiscent of the sound made by rattlesnakes.

It lives in dry, stony localities, in deep, shady valleys with streams running through them and in roadside ditches. It is not to be found at altitudes above 600 metres. It hibernates from the beginning of November until mid-April. In June the female lays 2—5 eggs in holes in the ground. The newly-hatched young measure 30—35 cm.

The Leopard Snake has a typical V-shaped spot on its head and conspicuous black-ringed spots on its body (1). When newly hatched, the young may already have spots (2), or may have red stripes running along the length of their body (3). In adulthood the stripes

either break up into spots, or persist and form an individual colour aberration (which is comparatively rare, however).

North America abounds in species of the genus *Elaphe,* but what is surprising is that they have produced forms similar to

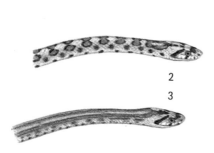

2

3

those in Europe — a phenomenon known as parallel evolution. For example, the Corn Snake, *E. guttata* (4), which occurs in the United States, is an almost complete replica of the handsomely coloured Leopard Snake. The young, however, differ, since in the American species they are greyish-blue with dark spots.

4

1

Four-lined Snake
Elaphe quatuorlineata   Colubridae

The Four-lined Snake is one of the largest European snakes and may occasionally attain a length of 250 cm. Its total length is emphasized by its powerful, muscular body. The impression of strength is further heightened by the relatively large scales on its back, each of which is distinctly ribbed.

The Four-lined Snake occurs in steppeland, semiarid localities overgrown with shrubs, or on the fringes of open deciduous woods. This diurnal snake hides in rodent burrows, deep crevices and piles of stones. It is usually to be found on the ground, but it can climb trees and rob birds' nests of both eggs and young. Otherwise it feeds mainly on rodents. Being so large, it also hunts large prey, including rodents up to the size of a rat and birds up to the size of a turtledove. In Macedonia the shock of capture caused one such snake to disgorge a turtledove, a young magpie and a small tortoise. Nowhere is the Four-lined Snake common, but it is not at all timid and it does not try to bite when disturbed. In July and August the female lays 6 — 16 eggs about 60 mm long and the young hatch in September or at the beginning of October.

The Four-lined Snake, in five subspecies, inhabits south-eastern Europe and the western part of Asia. *Elaphe quatuorlineata quatuorlineata* lives in Italy, Sicily, Yugoslavia, Albania, the south of Bulgaria, mainland Greece and the Cycades. The other widely distributed subspecies, *E. q. sauromates,* extends from Bulgaria to the Caucasus, Asia Minor and Iran. The other subspecies occupy small isolated islands of territory.

2

The nominate subspecies, *Elaphe quatuorlineata quatuorlineata* (1), has four lines running down its back — hence its Latin and its common name. In *E. q. sauromates* (2), the lines are replaced by rows of spots. The ground colour is very variable and ranges from yellow, through orange, to various shades of brown. The belly is always lighter in colour. Old

individuals display smaller colour
contrast and may actually be unicoloured.
  One of the biggest species of *Elaphe*
living in North America is the Black Rat
Snake, *E. obsoleta,* which can measure
over 250 cm. Its various subspecies are
very differently coloured. The Yellow Rat
Snake, *E. o. quadrivittata* (3), resembles
the Four-lined Snake.

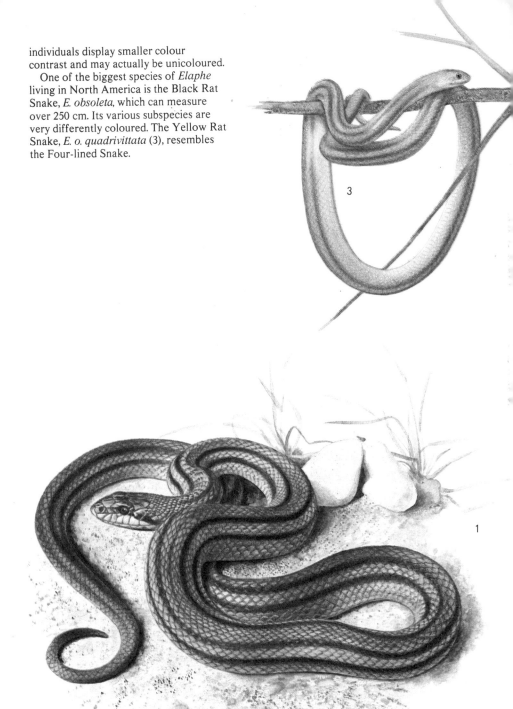

3

1

Aesculapian Snake
Elaphe longissima

Colubridae

The specific name of this species (*longissima* — longest) is fully justified as far as central Europe is concerned. Here it attains a length of up to 200 cm, but in more northerly regions it reaches only 160 cm.

It has two European subspecies. *Elaphe longissima longissima* is to be found from north-eastern Spain, across central and southern Europe, as far as Iran, and *E. l. romana* extends from central Italy to Sicily.

This snake takes its vernacular name from Aesculapius (or Asklepios), the Roman (initially Greek) god of healing and medicine, to whom the snake was dedicated in ancient Greece. From Rome, the cult spread over the whole of Europe, in the train of the Roman armies.

The Aesculapian Snake inhabits warm wooded grasslands and small leafy woods, rocky localities and often deserted or derelict buildings. It is both active and graceful and is also able to climb bushes and trees, where it occasionally seeks its food. It hunts during the warm part of the day, chiefly in the afternoon. Otherwise it hides in a hole in a tree, or coils itself up on a shady branch. In addition to voles and mice it catches moles, lizards and nestlings, suffocating its prey by constriction. At the end of June or the beginning of July the female lays 5—8 elongate eggs measuring about 45 mm in a hole in a tree or a tree stump. The young, which measure about 12 cm, hatch in September, when the adult snakes are already preparing for hibernation. They reappear in the spring, in April or May.

The Aesculapian Snake (1) is usually a uniform yellowish to blackish-brown colour with a lighter belly. Young specimens (2) can be distinguished from adult animals by the light collar-like marks behind their head and the traces of reticulation formed by the light edges of their body scales.

2

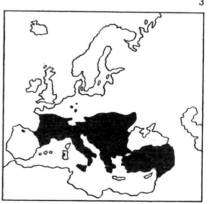

3

1

In southern Europe the Aesculapian
Snake is distributed over a continuous
area, but in the north it occurs in isolated
pockets (3). At one time it was thought to
have been introduced to these regions,
but nowadays, following palaeontological
findings, it is generally believed that these
pockets are the sole remains of a once
extensive area which was progressively
reduced by movements of the icesheet.

Ladder Snake
Elaphe scalaris
Colubridae

The Ladder Snake inhabits coastal regions of the Iberian Peninsula, France, the Iles d'Hyères and Minorca. It can attain a length of 160 cm, but generally does not measure more than 120 cm.

Like other members of this genus, it favours sunny localities. Stony slopes with only occasional bushes are a typical habitat, but it can also be found in deserted orchards, old vineyards and open leafy woods or on dry rocks. It hunts almost entirely during the daytime. At night and in bad weather it shelters in a rodent burrow, a pile of stones or a hollow tree. It is very quick and agile and bites fiercely if picked up. It feeds mainly on warm-blooded vertebrates and climbs right to the top of trees to raid birds' nests.

The mating season is in May or June. The 6—12 elongate white eggs are laid between the end of June and August and the young hatch in September or October. At first they live chiefly on small lizards, but they also eat various insects, such as small grasshoppers or crickets.

This snake takes its name from the markings of the young, which have dark bars across them, resembling the rungs of a ladder (Latin *scalae, scalarum* = ladder). Adult specimens are usually an inconspicuous shade of brown or grey, with two more or less pronounced stripes running down their back and with a dark spot behind each eye (the spots are sometimes absent). The belly is usually yellowish or ochre.

The Ladder Snake (1) is one of the more modestly coloured members of the genus. It kills its prey by constriction (2). The coils are so tight that the victim is suffocated in much the same way as the prey of boas and pythons.

Snakes' internal organs (3) are adapted to the shape of their extremely long body. Usually only the long right lobe of the lung is developed, and the left lobe is reduced. The heart is similar to that of lizards. Both the stomach and the kidneys have lengthened in the direction of the body axis. There is no bladder. Paired organs do not lie side by side, but one behind the other, so as not to increase the circumference of the body. Paired masses of fatty tissue, called fat bodies, together with a slow metabolic rate, enable the snake to go for a long time without food.

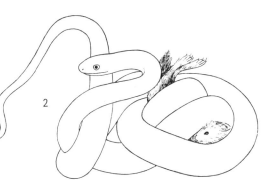

2

1

Hohenacker's Snake
Elaphe hohenackeri

Colubridae

This snake is a typical inhabitant of mountains and foothils, where it is found in a variety of habitats from dry slopes with sparse vegetation to the moist valleys of rivers and streams. It has even been encountered in the heart of dense forests on the one hand, and in the immediate vicinity of human communities (in gardens, fields and vineyards) on the other. Here it seeks shelter in mounds of stones or in stone walls. In the mountains it ascends to an altitude of 2,500 metres.

With a length of 75 cm it is one of the smallest *Elaphe* species. At the end of June or in July the female lays up to seven eggs about 40 mm long, and the young hatch out about a month later.

The Rat Snake, *Elaphe dione,* is another small species, with an exceptionally large area of distribution reaching from the southern Ukraine to the shores of the Pacific in the Far East. It is a pretty little snake measuring only a metre in length. It has a preference for steppeland, but can also be found high up in the mountains — as high as 3,500 metres. It feeds on a variety of other animals, including small mammals, birds, lizards, snakes, frogs and toads. It even ventures into the sea to catch fish. It crushes birds' eggs in a similar way to that of the African Egg-eating Snake, *Dasypeltis scabra,* with vertebral processes projecting into its gullet. The female lays 5—16 eggs in July or August.

The genus *Elaphe* comprises about 50 species distributed in Europe, Asia and North and Central America. They are distinguished by a muscular body and by the sharp edges of their notched abdominal scales. The purpose of this latter character seems to be to help them to climb smooth tree trunks or the roughly plastered walls of houses.

3

190

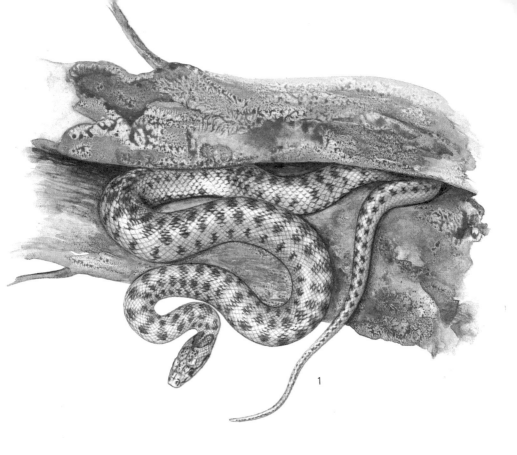

1

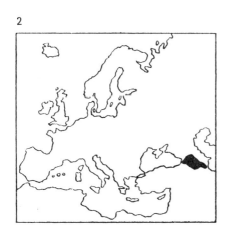

2

The area of distribution of Hohenacker's Snake has its centre in Asia Minor and from here it stretches to north-western Iran, Transcaucasia and the eastern Caucasus (where it is rare, however). Its isolated incidence in the mountains of southern Lebanon, where the subspecies *Elaphe hohenackeri taurica* has been described, is of zoogeographical interest.

The nominate subspecies, *E. h. hohenackeri* (1), occupies a very small part of Europe in the eastern Caucasus (2).

Elaphe dione (3) occurs most frequently in the typical form, but occasionally dark-coloured specimens are found. It manifests fear or displeasure by means of quick vibrations of its tail, which, among dry leaves, sound rather like the rattle of a rattlesnake.

191

Grass Snake
Natrix natrix
Colubridae

This most common of all European snakes is to be found beside rivers, marshes and pools and in cultivated country in the vicinity of lakes and ponds. It is so familiar that the very word 'snake' immediately conjures up in the lay mind an image of this species with the characteristic crescent-shaped spots behind its head.

The area of distribution of this snake stretches from north Africa, across almost the whole of Europe, to the Sea of Aral in Asia. It is found in low-lying country, along the seashores, and in mountains to an altitude of 2,000 metres. It is a timid snake. If picked up it seldom tries to bite, but it can emit an unpleasant odour produced by a secretion from a special gland beside the cloaca, and this is its main defence.

It feeds on various amphibians, fishes and — very occasionally — mammals encountered near the water. The young also catch invertebrates (mainly earthworms). The Grass Snake, though not very fast, is a persevering swimmer.

Grass snakes spend the winter in rock fissures, deep rodent burrows, hollow trees and other similar shelters, often at a considerable distance from water. They usually hibernate in small groups, frequently in company with other species. With the first rays of the spring sun — sometimes as early as March — they emerge again. In summer the females lay up to 50 white, longish eggs measuring about 26 × 18 mm. The young, which hatch in about two months, depending on the temperature, are 15—19 cm long. Several females often lay their eggs in the same place.

The Grass Snake can attain a length of 150 cm, but the males are usually smaller and even the females are generally only about 100 cm long. Altogether, there are nine subspecies spread over its total area. *Natrix natrix natrix* (1) occurs from the Rhine to Siberia and from Scandinavia to the north of the Balkans. *N. n. persa* (2) lives between the southern part of central Europe and the Caspian Sea, *N. n. scutata* lives to the east of the river Dnieper, *N. n. helvetica* inhabits England and stretches across the Alps to Italy and Istria, *N. n. astreptophora* (3) is known in the Iberian Peninsula, Morocco and Algeria. The last four species inhabit islands — *N. n. cetti* Sardinia, *N. n. corsa* Corsica, *N. n. sicula* Sicily (and Calabria) and *N. n. schweizeri* the Cyclades. The various subspecies differ in their colouring and markings and the plates on the head.

3

2

1

193

Viperine Snake
Natrix maura

Colubridae

The members of the genus *Natrix* are distributed over a large part of the globe. Most species live in the temperate belt and a few are found in tropical regions. It is interesting to note that, whereas all European species are oviparous, North American species give birth to live young.

The Viperine Snake is very variably coloured. Its markings and behaviour give it a resemblance to a true viper. If in danger it adopts an offensive pose and strikes at its attacker, usually with its mouth closed. Like all the members of the genus *Natrix*, it is a typically aquatic snake and can be encountered near ponds, rivers and mountain streams and even in brackish water. In the mountains it is not to be seen above 1,400 metres. It swims extremely well and catches most of its food (fish, amphibians and amphibian larvae) in the water. The young also devour earthworms.

Mating takes place in March or April. In June the female lays up to 20 eggs measuring about 26 × 18 mm in loose soil or under stones and the young, which measure 20 cm, hatch in August.

No subspecies of this snake have been described. The variability of its colouring is within the framework of the species and has no great systematic significance.

Down its back the Viperine Snake has a zigzag row of spots very similar to the markings of a viper (1). It occurs on the Iberian Peninsula, the Balearic Islands and Sardinia and is abundant in north-western Africa (5 — shaded). Northern Italy is its most northerly limit. The region from here eastwards belongs to the related Tessellated Snake (5 — stippled). It is interesting that where the two areas overlap (5 — black), specimens of the Viperine Snake are found which look more like tessellated snakes. This is evidently the dividing line between two branches stemming from the same extinct ancestor.

The main features distinguishing harmless European colubrid snakes from vipers are to be found on the heads of these snakes. On the top of the head of colubrid snakes are a few large, regular plates (3), whereas a viper has more numerous, small and usually irregularly arranged plates (4). In vipers, the supraorbital scale forms a pronounced ridge. There is also a difference in the shape of the pupils, vipers having vertical, elliptical or slit-like pupils and colubrid snakes round pupils.

The popular Common Water Snake, *Natrix sipedon* (2), which inhabits the United States, is viviparous. In captivity it has been known to give birth to 58 young.

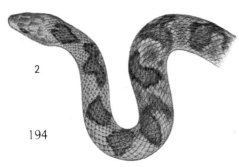

2

194

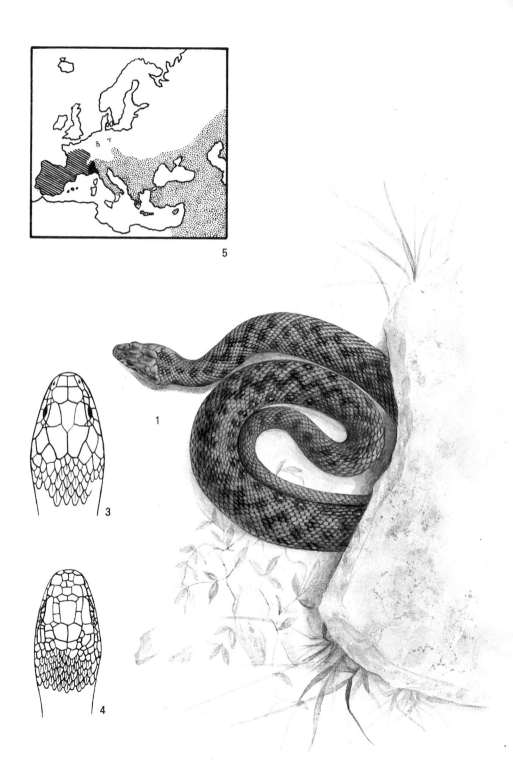

5

3

1

4

Dice Snake
Natrix tessellata

Colubridae

In Europe, no snake is so closely associated with water as the Dice Snake, which seldom moves more than a matter of a few metres from its element. It is most likely to be seen in shallow water, where it lurks in wait for the small fishes which constitute its sole food. It is an excellent diver and can remain beneath the surface for as long as 15 minutes.

It occurs in south-eastern Europe, Asia Minor and central Asia. In the north-western part of its area there are a few isolated colonies exclusively in river valleys with rocky sides. Here the heat-retaining rocks give rise to a specific microclimate with the warmth essential for the existence of this snake. In southern Europe it inhabits large lakes and is found along the coasts. Central Asian populations live beside small mountain torrents in loess mountains. In some places the Dice Snake even frequents thermal waters. Quite often it congregates in large numbers.

These snakes mate in May or June and in June or July the females lay 10 — 25 leathery eggs, mainly in piles of organic debris washed up by the water, or in loose soil under stones. The eggs resemble those of the Grass Snake and are similarly joined together by strings of a mucoid substance. The young, which hatch at the beginning of September, measure up to 24 cm.

The Dice Snake hibernates from October to April in holes in the ground in dry places close to water. It has one disagreeable habit. If picked up, it empties its gut at a tremendous rate, to the accompaniment of an evil-smelling odour emanating from the secretions of its scent glands. The concomitant hissing is an effective, but purely passive, defence reflex, since the snake never bites.

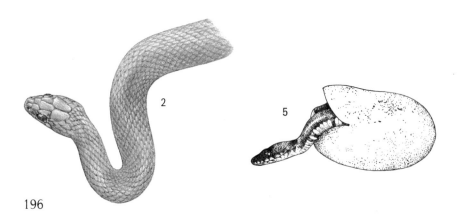

2

5

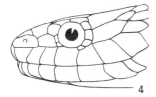

3

4

The Dice Snake has no yellow crescents behind its head and the dark spots on its belly are arranged in a chequered pattern. The snake is about 110 cm long and is very variably coloured. A spotted greyish-green form is the commonest in central Europe (1). In southern Europe, completely black specimens or a straw coloured form with a red belly (2) are frequent. Individuals from the extreme north of the distribution area of this snake have fewer plates on their head — two preocular and three postocular (3). Southwards and eastwards the number increases, the full number being three preocular and four postocular plates (4). This feature is subject to variability and thus cannot be regarded as taxonomically important.

Newly-hatched dice snakes are coloured and marked in the same way as their parents (5).

1

Smooth Snake
Coronella austriaca
Colubridae

The area of this simply, but elegantly coloured snake extends from the Ural Mountains to the northern half of the Iberian Peninsula, Great Britain and Scandinavia. The head is only indistinctly divided from the body and the whole snake does not measure more than 80 cm. The Smooth Snake is active during the daytime and hunts in the early evening only at the height of summer. It feeds mainly on lizards and snakes, including young vipers, and if it comes across a burrow containing young rodents, it devours them too. Since these snakes have been found in bushes at nesting time, it is thought that nestlings are also part of their diet. Before devouring its victims, the Smooth Snake smothers them in its coils.

This snake inhabits grasslands and wooded steppes, and is most often found on the edges of forests, in hedges, in rubble at the foot of steep rocks, on bare outcrops and even in gardens. It is never found in groups, like members of the genus *Natrix,* for example, and its sober protective colouring makes it very difficult to see.

In April the snakes leave their winter quarters and mate. Smooth snakes are ovoviviparous. The eggs remain in the body of the female until the young are fully developed, and these are born the instant the egg membranes rupture, usually at the end of the summer. The young number up to 15 and measure 12.5—18 cm. Sometimes the female gives birth to several young and then lays eggs, from which the young snakes emerge a few seconds later.

The Smooth Snake begins hibernation in September or October, depending on the weather.

4

The Smooth Snake (1) is notable for its glossy appearance, for which its smooth scales, typical of the genus *Coronella* (2) as distinct from the ridged scales of the genus *Natrix* (3), are responsible.

If taken by surprise, and unable to escape, the Smooth Snake often shows aggression. First it adopts a defensive pose, raising and withdrawing its head, which widens behind the eyes (4). It utters warning hisses and, if the enemy still approaches, it strikes very rapidly and attempts to bite. If the attempt is successful, it usually hangs on, since its tiny recurved teeth (5) refuse to let go. Although its bite is not dangerous in

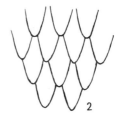

itself, the small, bleeding wounds need to be treated to prevent them from being infected by any food left in the snake's mouth.

Its warning pose and the configuration of the spots on the head and neck are somewhat reminiscent of a viper and a frightened human is therefore more likely to kill the animal outright rather than wait and take a closer look.

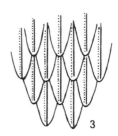

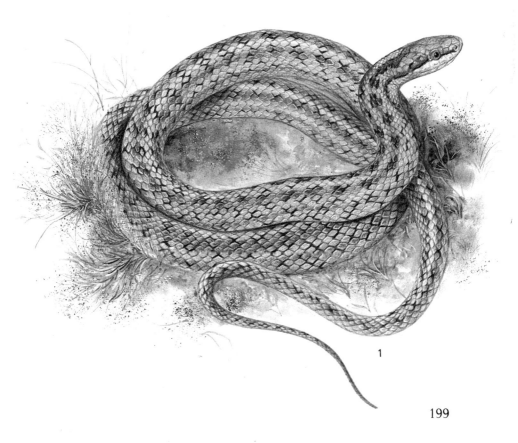

Southern Smooth Snake
Coronella girondica   Colubridae

This snake, which is closely related to the Smooth Snake, inhabits the western part of Austria, Italy, Sicily, the south of France, the Iberian Peninsula and north-west Africa. Unlike the preceding species it forms no geographical subspecies. Although the areas of the two species overlap, no hybrids have been described, since they both reproduce in different ways, the Southern Smooth Snake being oviparous and the Smooth Snake ovoviviparous. The Southern Smooth Snake mates in April or May and the young, usually about five in number, hatch in August or September. The young closely resemble the young of the Smooth Snake, including the red belly. After their first moult they catch small lizards and according to some authors they also devour insects.

The Southern Smooth Snake is essentially a lowland snake, but has several times been found at altitudes up to 1,500 metres (and in the Atlas Mountains in Morocco at 3,200 metres). It occurs mainly in stony but sunny localities with a sparse sprinkling of shrubs. It differs from the better-known Smooth Snake in moving more slowly, and having a more secretive mode of life. It also has a very different nature, for where the Smooth Snake is aggressive and does not hesitate to bite, if the Southern Smooth Snake is picked up it does its best to wriggle free and seldom bites.

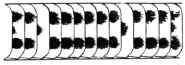

2

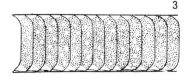

3

The Southern Smooth Snake (1) is generally yellow, grey, brown or reddish, with pronounced dark spots. It can measure 60—70 cm, but is usually smaller.

Adult individuals feed mainly on lizards and small snakes, including venomous species, but in captivity they also enjoy catching mice. They suffocate adult mice with their coils, in the same way as lizards, but swallow young rodents whole.

The biggest differences between the two species are in the marking on the underside of their body and the configuration of their head plates (the Southern Smooth Snake 2 and 4, Smooth Snake 3 and 5). The shape and size of their rostral plate are also different and

there are differences in the small plates on their upper jaw. In general, the Southern Smooth Snake can be considered an evolutionary older species, with more primitive characters.

Hooded Snake
Macroprotodon cucullatus
Colubridae

The amount of available information on the biology of this snake is relatively small. So far it has been found in central and southern parts of Portugal and Spain, on the Balearic Islands and Lampedusa and in Africa, north of the Sahara, between Morocco and Egypt. It always occurs in dry, stony, open localities with dry, loose soil.

The Hooded Snake is the only member of the genus. It leads a concealed existence, hidden away under stones, in holes, in the soil and in other shelters during the daytime, and it emerges only in the evening. Its main prey comprises various species of lizards, which it attacks while they are asleep. It paralyses its prey with the venom fangs at the back of its jaw. Its venom is virtually harmless to man, but in any case humans are not likely to be bitten, since the small jaws cannot be opened very wide and the snake often makes no attempt to bite. This snake sometimes displays unexpected agility, and if taken by surprise, it jerks its head back, showing the underside, and then makes for shelter as quickly as possible.

The female lays 5−7 markedly elongate eggs, which she hides in sandy soil under warmed stones.

The classification of this species has not been fully elucidated. Despite the variability of its colouring, some authors maintain that it forms no subspecies. There is some uncertainty, however, over the population in the south-east of Morocco, which has rows of 23−25 scales across its body, whereas the usual number is only 19−23.

The Hooded Snake is one of the smallest European snakes, the longest so far known measuring 65 cm, but something under 50 cm being the normal length. Behind the head are blackish-brown markings like a collar (2), which sometimes extend to the crown of the head (1). Some specimens have no distinctive markings, however.

4

2

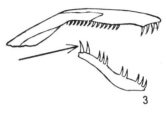

In North America, the colubrid snakes of the genus *Hypsiglena* are similar to *Macroprotodon*. The most familiar, the Night Snake, *H. torquata* (4), measures only about 40 cm and lives mainly on lizards.

Colubrid snakes may have poison teeth (3) separated by a clearly discernible space, in the back of their jaw. There are usually one to three teeth in each half of the jaw.

3

1

European Cat Snake
Telescopus fallax
Colubridae

Of all 11 species of the genus *Telescopus* (known also under the name *Tarbophis*), only one lives in Europe. The European Cat Snake inhabits the Balkan Peninsula, the Aegean and Mediterranean islands, the Caucasus, Asia Minor and Arabia. It forms a total of seven subspecies, only three of which occur in Europe — *T. f. fallax* in the Balkans, on Malta and the Cyclades and in Asia Minor, *T. f. squamatus* on the island of Kufonesi to the south-east of Malta and *T. f. pallidus* on Crete and a few of the neighbouring islands.

The European Cat Snake can be encountered in warm, dry stony localities. In the south of its range it ascends to an altitude 1,800 metres, but is normally to be found at lower levels. During the daytime it shelters under large stones, in crevices or in stone walls and hunts early in the morning or after dusk. It lives almost entirely on small lizards. Prey is killed or paralysed by a bite from the venom teeth in the back of the mouth. The poison is not dangerous to humans, but it kills small lizards in 2−3 minutes.

The snakes mate in early spring and at the end of June or the beginning of July the female lays 6−9 eggs measuring about 12 × 30 mm. The young, which hatch in September, are 15−20 cm long. At first they live on insects, which they catch at night.

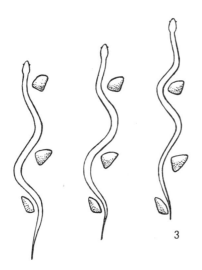

3

The European Cat Snake (1) attains a length of about 100 cm. It is a very active and agile animal. When in danger it coils itself into a flat disc, hisses loudly and tries to bite, but its venom fangs are relatively short. Even if one is actually bitten there is no need for medical attention.

Its colouring is very variable. The eye, with a vertical pupil (2) which widens to an ellipse in poor light, testifies to its nocturnal mode of life.

In snakes, the free ends of the ribs take over the role of limbs in locomotion and

act as a support. Snakes also make use of irregularities in the terrain to support themselves (3). On smooth or loose ground, such as sand, their body undulates in wide loops (4). The plates on the belly and sides of a snake are also important for locomotion. The plates and the free ends of the ribs are joined together by muscles, the movements of which push the plates backwards and forwards, while the ribs remain rigid. This technique is used for forward movement in a straight line or for climbing.

Orsini's Viper
Vipera ursinii   Viperidae

Orsini's Viper is the smallest European viper, its average length being 40 cm, and its maximum length 60 cm. It occurs in a few small isolated areas, often at considerable distances from one another. Individual populations display marked differences and have therefore been described as subspecies. In conformity with its size, Orsini's Viper has small venom fangs, a small poison gland and only a small amount of poison, so that it is the viper least dangerous to humans. Some zoologists handle it with no more protection than a pair of leather gloves. In addition, it is rare and it is placid by nature.

Vipera ursinii renardi stands somewhat apart from the other subspecies, partly because it is distributed over a large coherent area which, in the east, stretches far beyond the borders of Europe. It is sometimes abundant in the places where it occurs. Some subspecies are to be found at both low and high altitudes, while others are known only in the mountains. *V. u. rakosiensis* has always been found in open meadows, where vipers are not normally expected to be encountered. In Hungary it was last found between the Danube and Tisa rivers. Here single specimens appeared on low sandy mounds surrounded by damp meadows, where the only shelter was in rodent burrows. This snake does not tolerate high temperatures and is only seen in daytime in early spring. Later it changes to a nocturnal mode of life.

In September the female gives birth to up to six live young measuring only 12 cm.

3

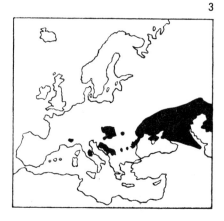

Orsini's Viper (1) differs from other European vipers as regards its biology and its ecological requirements. The composition of its diet is very interesting. Observation of the subspecies *V.u.rakosiensis* under natural conditions confirmed that they lived mainly on insects, especially *Orthoptera* (2). Sand lizards whose tails were in varying stages of regeneration occurred in localities with

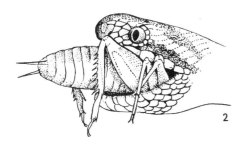

a high concentration of these vipers. When hunting, young snakes catch lizards by the tail, which is immediately shed and devoured by the snake. The Saddled Leaf-nosed Snake, *Phyllorhynchus browni*, of North America uses similar tactics, its young consuming the tails of the Banded Gecko, *Coleonyx variegatus*.

The small, isolated areas of Orsini's Viper in Europe represent the remains of a once coherent area (3) and is evidence that this now rare snake is in danger of becoming extinct.

2

1

Adder, Common Viper
Vipera berus
Viperidae

The Adder or Common Viper is a familiar snake with relatively few explicit environmental requirements. It is to be found in low-lying country, at altitudes up to 3,000 metres, on the edges of woods, in clearings, in peat-bogs, in hedgerows and in the vicinity of water. It always remains in the same spot, so the same individual can be encountered in a particular place for years.

The Adder usually measures about 60 cm and even the biggest specimens do not exceed 80 cm. In early spring and in the autumn the Adder basks in the sun for the greater part of each day, but in summer it becomes an animal of twilight and night, and spends only a short time in the sun. Its diet consists mainly of small rodents, frogs and toads, but at nesting time young birds fall prey to this snake. It also catches lizards (particularly viviparous lizards). The Adder shelters in vole burrows, in piles of stones and beneath roots (especially under bushes). It swims very well and can cross wide rivers and lakes.

Mating takes place in the spring and after three months the female gives birth to 8—12 young measuring about 16 cm. A single litter can include both young and eggs, from which the young hatch as soon as the eggs have been laid. In the northern part of its area the Adder does not breed every year. The young live on earthworms, insects and small lizards.

Adders generally hibernate singly or in small groups, but occasionally groups numbering several hundred have been known. Hibernation lasts from about October to April, according to the weather.

The bite of an adder is not dangerous for human beings unless the venom is injected directly into the blood stream. Immediate medical attention is nevertheless always essential.

3

The Adder inhabits practically the whole of Europe except for the south of France, the greater part of the Iberian Peninsula, southern Italy and the south-eastern part of the Balkan Peninsula. It also lives in Great Britain and beyond the Arctic Circle. In the east its area extends to the coast of the Pacific Ocean. The nominate subspecies *Vipera berus berus* inhabits a vast territory stretching from Great Britain to the river Amur. *V. b. bosniensis* lives in the mountains of the Balkan

Peninsula and *V. b. sachalinensis* on the island of Sakhalin. The precise classification of an isolated population in the north-west of the Iberian Peninsula is in some doubt. Though sometimes referred to as *V. b. seoanei,* according to contemporary opinion it is a new species, *Vipera seoanei.*

Male adders (1) are generally more vividly marked than the largely russet red females (2). Plain red or black (3), specimens without any markings are sometimes found.

1 ♂

2 ♀

Asp Viper
Vipera aspis
Viperidae

The Asp Viper is a snake of the mountains of south, south-west and western central Europe. It lives both in hilly country and high up in the mountains, at altitudes up to 2,600 metres. Its haunts are warmer than those of the Adder and it is more likely to be encountered on dry, stony slopes or in open mountain meadows. It inhabits the same territory for the whole of its life.

Although some individuals may measure up to 75 cm, its average length is about 60 cm. There is no difficulty in distinguishing the sex of adult specimens, since the males are longer, slimmer and more vividly marked than the generally lighter-coloured females.

These snakes hibernate in crevices in rocks, in caves and in underground caverns, emerging in March or April to mate. Toward the end of summer the female gives birth to 4—18 young measuring 18—20 cm, which at first live mainly on lizards and insects. Adult individuals live almost entirely on small rodents or insectivores. Sexual maturity is attained after four years, when the snakes measure about 50 cm.

The Asp Viper is primarily diurnal. In spring and autumn it is active the whole day long, but in summer, especially in the noonday heat, it hides away under stones.

The area of the Halys Viper, *Agkistrodon halys,* the only pit viper in eastern Europe, reaches all the way to China and Japan. It forms about four subspecies and measures 70 cm.

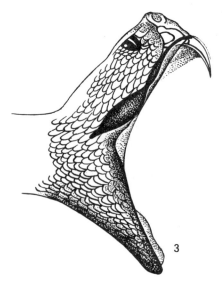

3

Although the area of distribution of the Asp Viper is not particularly large, long-term isolation in mountain localities has resulted in the formation of six subspecies differing in ground colour and in the pattern of the spots on their back. *Vipera aspis aspis* (1) is less distinctively marked than the reddish coloured *V. a. hugyi* (2) in Sicily and Calabria.

Snakes do not attack anywhere near as swiftly as is generally supposed. For

1

2

instance, the maximum rate of attack of a viper is about 3 metres per second, while a human hand strikes at 6, a trained boxer at 12 metres per second. Of course, a snake's attack is intensified by the element of surprise and the small distance involved. The venom fangs are not erected until the last phase, when the mouth is opened (3), and after the attack they are folded back again.

Snub-nosed Viper
Vipera latasti   Viperidae

The Snub-nosed Viper is usually about 60 cm long, but may occasionally measure up to 75 cm. It inhabits rocky areas in hilly country and open woods. In the European part of its range — which is confined to the Iberian Peninsula — it is to be found at altitudes up to 1,300 metres. The subspecies *Vipera latasti monticola,* which lives in the Atlas Mountains in North Africa, occurs up to 4,000 metres.

This species is biologically similar to the Nose-horned Viper and the Asp Viper. The female gives birth to 2—6 young, which live on lizards and small invertebrate animals.

The Caucasus Viper, *Vipera kaznakovi,* a species with a very limited range, is one of the rarest European vipers. Outside Europe, in Turkey, it lives at low altitudes, but in the European part of its area, in the western Caucasus, it lives at altitudes above 2,000 metres. Here it frequents rocky wooded hillsides, subalpine meadows and stone-covered slopes overgrown with ferns.

Little is known of the biology of *V. kaznakovi,* but it certainly does not tolerate high temperatures. It warms itself for a short time early in the morning and when the temperature rises above 15 °C it seeks shelter in the labyrinth of spaces among the stones. It feeds mainly on orthopterous insects, which abound in such places, but it never despises small rodents and lizards.

The sex of most vipers can be determined from the shape and length of the tail. In females it is short and tapers off gradually from the cloaca to the tip, while in males it narrows abruptly at the cloaca and is long and thin.

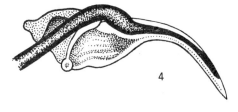

4

With a horn at the tip of its snout, the Snub-nosed Viper (1) closely resembles the Nose-horned Viper. The two cannot be mistaken for each other, however, since nowhere do they occur together.

The vivid colours and markings on the body of the Caucasus Viper are very variable (2). On its back there are either conspicuous stripes or paterns, both providing good camouflage among the twisted leaves of dry ferns.

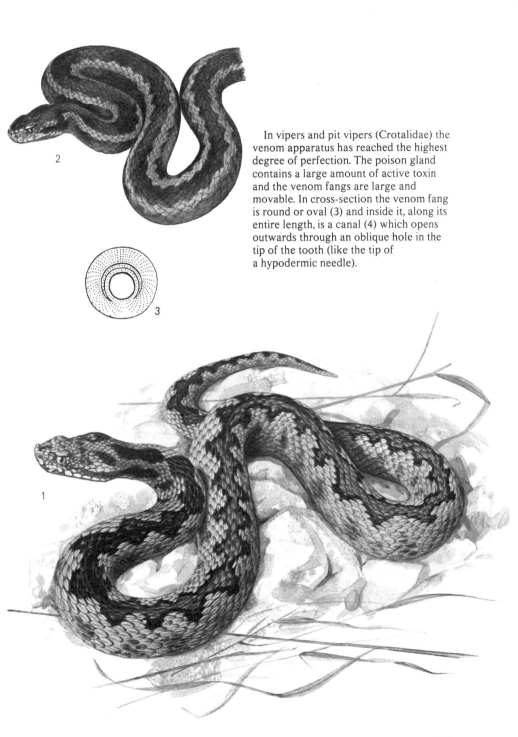

2

In vipers and pit vipers (Crotalidae) the venom apparatus has reached the highest degree of perfection. The poison gland contains a large amount of active toxin and the venom fangs are large and movable. In cross-section the venom fang is round or oval (3) and inside it, along its entire length, is a canal (4) which opens outwards through an oblique hole in the tip of the tooth (like the tip of a hypodermic needle).

3

1

Nose-horned Viper
Vipera ammodytes   Viperidae

This is one of the viperine snakes the bite of which can be very dangerous for human beings. Its average length is 60—80 cm, but specimens a metre long are occasionally found. The venom fangs measure over 5 mm, so the poison is injected deep into the tissues and takes effect quickly. Not only is the venom more effective than that of the Adder, but there is also about four times as much of it. However, like all venomous snakes, this one uses its poison sparingly and never empties both its poison glands at once.

The Nose-horned Viper inhabits a large area in south-eastern Europe and western Asia. Everywhere it is found in the same type of habitat — a dry and sunny locality with stony ground and not too much vegetation. In the mountains it ascends to heights above 2,000 metres, but it may equally well be encountered on the seashore. It never occurs on sand dunes, however.

In Europe, the first males emerge from hibernation at the end of March or the beginning of April, while the females generally appear about a fortnight later. The snakes mate chiefly in May and the young are usually born after 3—4 months. The average number of young is about ten, but the actual number varies from four to 20 depending on the size and age of the female. The newborn snakes measure 15—20 cm. Like all young vipers, they are venomous from birth. After their first moult they begin to look for food, which in the case consists mainly of small lizards or young mammals. Adult snakes feed chiefly on mammals of an appropriate size and occasionally catch lizards, birds and other snakes.

The Nose-horned Viper hibernates in rock fissures or in underground cavities, often in large numbers. Groups of several dozen hibernating snakes are no rarity.

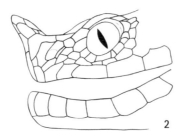

2

1

214

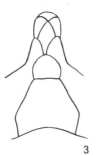

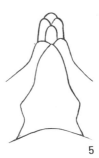

3   4   5

The Nose-horned Viper (1) forms a total of six subspecies over its very wide area. All possess the characteristic protuberance on the tip of the nose (2), but differ as regards colouring, head plates and size. Differences between the plates on the snout are illustrated in fig. 3—5 (seen from above). The possibility of cross-breeding between subspecies and resultant intermediate forms cannot be ruled out. *Vipera ammodytes ammodytes* (3) inhabits the area bounded by Italy, Austria, Rumania, Bulgaria and Yugoslavia, *V. a. meridionalis* (4) occurs in Albania, the south of Bulgaria, Yugoslavia, Greece and Asia Minor, *V. a. montandoni* (5) comes from Rumania and Bulgaria, *V. a. transcaucasiana* from the Caucasus and Anatolia and *V. a. ruffoi* is found in the mountains of the Alto Adige in Italy. The last subspecies, *V. a. gregorwallneri,* lives in northern Yugoslavia and in Austria.

Ottoman Viper
Vipera xanthina Viperidae

The area of distribution of this robust snake centres on Asia Minor. The nominate subspecies, *Vipera xanthina xanthina,* is found in Europe only on the southern coast of the European part of Turkey and on a few islands in the Aegean. *V. x. palestinae* is known in Jordan, Israel and Syria, where it lives in hills and mountains up to an altitude of 2,000 metres, being found mainly on loose stony ground, though sometimes on cultivated land, on pastureland and even near marshes.

It is mainly nocturnal, but can also be encountered during the daytime. It hunts small rodents and birds. Its highly active toxin ranks it, together with the Blunt-nosed Viper and the Nose-horned Viper, among the most dangerous European snakes. It is rare, however, and cases of humans being bitten are not very numerous.

In March or April the snakes emerge from hibernation and mate soon afterwards. The young, measuring about 20 cm, are born at the end of August or the beginning of September. Their diet consists mainly of lizards, young rodents and grasshoppers.

This snake can measure up to 120 cm and its size enables it to attack from a greater distance than other European vipers. Its reactions are unpredictable and its bite can prove fatal, if untreated.

The Ottoman Viper is a phylogenetically advanced species, as a glance at the minute plates, all roughly the same size, on the top of its head indicates. In more primitive vipers, such as Orsini's Viper and the Adder, some of the plates in the pileus are larger than the others.

The marking on the head and body of *Vipera xanthina xanthina* (1) are so characteristic that it cannot be mistaken for any other European species. Transcaucasian localities with an incidence of the subspecies *V. x. raddei* (2) come close to the borders of eastern Europe. This subspecies differs markedly from the nominate form and some experts regard it as a separate species, Radde's Viper, *V. raddei.* It inhabits mountains at altitudes of 1,000 — 2,500 metres, where it frequents stony slopes. In pastureland it is found near piles of large stones, under which it seeks both shelter and food. It is unusual for people to be bitten by this snake, since the places it frequents lie in very thinly populated regions.

There are no true vipers in North America, but pit vipers of the family Crotalidae are widely distributed. Among them is the Eastern Diamond-back Rattlesnake, *Crotalus adamanteus* (3), a large snake, responsible for many deaths. Its rattle — loosely connected horny segments at the end of its tail — is shown in Fig. 4.

3

Blunt-nosed Viper
Vipera lebetina
Viperidae

As well as being the largest Europen viper, this snake is also one of the largest members of the genus *Vipera*. In exceptional cases it attains a length of 200 cm and a weight of over 5 kg, but it is generally smaller. Its bite is exceedingly dangerous, since its teeth remain embedded in the tissue and the masticating movements of the jaws pump a large amount of poison into the wounds. Most vipers bite very rapidly, and immediately withdraw their teeth again.

The Blunt-nosed Viper inhabits a wide range of habitats over a large area. It is to be found on stony hillsides, among shrubs, in grassy meadows and on dry, infertile ground. Despite its size and its apparent ungainliness it can climb trees very well. If disturbed, it hisses loudly and the lightning nature of its attack makes it all the more dangerous.

It feeds mainly on rodents and birds; the young generally devouring lizards. Mating takes place in April or May and at the end of summer the female lays 15−20 eggs, from which the young hatch some 40 days later.

In all, seven subspecies are known, most of them in Asia and northern Africa. *V. l. schweizeri* lives in Europe on Milos, Kimolos, Sifnos and a few other islands of the Cyclades. *V. l. obtusa* occurs in the Little Caucasus. This species has been studied in detail in the Shirvan Steppe in Azerbaijan and the surprising finding was made that in mild winters it availed itself of the modest warmth to bask in the sun near its collective winter quarters (rodent burrows, or piles of stones). It becomes active at temperatures of only 9−10 °C.

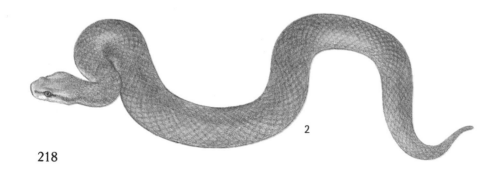

2

Vipera lebetina schweizeri is the smallest subspecies. It generally measures 60—80 cm and the males are always smaller than the females. Its tail terminates in a horny tip a few millimetres long. It is usually inconspicuously mottled (1), making it harder to see and consequently more dangerous. Plain light brownish-red individuals (2) are rare. The young are more brightly coloured and more vividly marked.

Very often, characteristic prick marks (3) appear on the skin of the victim after snakebite. The two rows of tiny pricks are caused by the normal teeth, the two larger ones by the venom fangs. Sometimes only one tooth is used, however, and sometimes only the wounds made by the venom fangs can be seen.

3

1

VENOM PRODUCTION

Practically all European amphibians have skin glands which produce a more or less active toxin. The toxin provides protection against some enemies, but does not prevent some predators from eating amphibians. The fact is that digestive juices can break down the toxin sufficiently to make it ineffective. Among the amphibians there are many species — especially among the tailless amphibians — which produce some of the most deadly animal poisons that exist. For example, South American Indians use the venom of the brightly marked members of the genus *Dendrobates* to tip their darts.

The only two venomous lizards are the Gila Monster and the Beaded Lizard from Central and North America, but because they are rare and retiring, and because they live in remote desert country, the number of people known to have been bitten by them is small. The Earless Monitor, a very rare species living in northern Borneo, is also said to be venomous.

Snakes form the largest group of venomous reptiles. They have the best-developed venom-conducting apparatus and the most effective poisons. The poison glands are modified salivary glands, and most snakes are equipped with them. In recent years it has been found that snakes previously considered to be non-venomous, like the Smooth Snake and the Grass Snake, also possess poison glands, but that the glands are enclosed in tissue and are ductless.

The poison glands are paired, that is to say, there is one on either side of the upper jaw. There are no poison glands in the lower jaw. The poison gland stretches well back behind the eye and in vipers and rattlesnakes it even stretches back beyond the neck. Round it are sphincter muscles which squirt the venom to the base of the venom canal or groove. In all snakes the venom fangs come out after a time or are broken, but new ones grow in their place. Quite often 'reserve' fangs grow before the old ones drop out and sometimes there may be several on either side of the jaw. In the Gaboon Viper, for instance, six venom teeth, one behind the other, have been found on either side.

Snake venom is usually dangerous only to the animals on which the snake feeds. When injected into such an animal, it not only causes death, but also quickly breaks down the tissues and thus helps to shorten the time required for digestion. Snake poisons are complex proteins, and the reaction of the victim's tissues are actually a reaction to a foreign protein. The basic ingredients of snake poisons are neurotoxins, which destroy the tissue of the central nervous system, haemorrhagins, which break down the endothelial cells lining the blood vessels, thrombins, which promote blood-clotting (they are the antithesis of antifibrins or anticoagulins, which delay clotting), haemolysins, which break down red blood cells, and cytolysins, which decompose white blood cells and tissue cells. Snake poisons also contain antibacterial substances and enzymes which promote the decomposition of the tissue of the victim and hasten its digestion. The venom of individual species or groups consists of the above components combined in different ways (though not all together) and in varying proportions.

The evaluation of the degree of venomousness of individual species is not without its problems. The amount, composition and effectiveness (toxicity) of the venom in the poison gland are important factors. Professional publications compare the effects of poisons by measuring the number of milligrammes of dry poison, diluted and injected subcutaneously, needed to kill mice weighing 100 g. According to this comparison, the most venomous snake in existence is the Beaked Sea Snake the venom of which is lethal for mice in a dosage of only 0.015 mg.

In snakebite, only about a third of the contents of the poison glands (but generally less) may be injected into the wound, since snakes use their venom sparingly. For a practical comparison of toxicity and danger to man, therefore, the maximum venom content of the poison glands is decisive. In this case an Australian snake, the Taipan, unquestionably takes the first place, since the contents of its paired poison glands would be capable of killing 80 people. The figures for Adder venom are in general favourable, the lethal dose for a human adult being 15 mg, while the glands seldom contain more than 10 mg.

The actual danger to man of any particular venomous European snake is impossible to evaluate, partly because different people react differently to the same amount of the same toxin and partly because the composition of the toxins of a number of rare venomous snakes is still unknown. The available data show that the bite of the Blunt-nosed Viper, the Ottoman Viper and the Nose-horned Viper can prove lethal. The bite of Orsini's Viper is relatively harmless, while the Halys and other vipers are moderately dangerous. The degree of toxicity of poisonous colubrid snakes is small.

FIRST AID FOR SNAKEBITE

Snakebite under European conditions should not be over-dramatized, but neither should it be underestimated. Medical attention should always be sought as soon as possible, but initially correct first aid should be given.

The first thing is not to panic, since fright can be communicated to the patient and result in shock. The next thing is to try to capture the snake, since its identification is important for the choice of antivenin. It also rules out any possibility of a harmless snake being mistaken for a venomous species. Incise the skin of the victim at the site of the bleeding tooth marks so as to stimulate the blood flow and thus wash more poison out of the wound. A knife or a razor blade sterilized over a flame makes the best instrument. The blood flow can be further accelerated by sucking the wound. (There must be no open wound in the mouth of the person rendering first aid). The affected limb should then be firmly bound with a bandage or a scarf just above the wound, i. e. on the side nearer the heart. Wire or cord should not be used, as they bruise the tissue. Nor should the bandage be so tight, that it prevents arterial blood from flowing through. At half-hourly intervals the bandage should be loosened for one or two minutes and then reapplied a little higher, and after 2—3 hours it can be removed altogether.

As soon as such first aid has been administered, the patient should see a doctor without further delay.

In some cases the bite of a snake with a comparatively weak toxin can be dangerous and require prompt medical attention — for example, if a child or a person allergic to animal poisons is bitten; if the upper half of the body (in particular the face or neck) is involved; if the venom fang has punctured a large blood vessel. In such cases there is danger in delay.

Similarly, the effect of toad or salamander toxins on the mucous membranes, especially of the eye, must never be underestimated. Every time an amphibian is handled, the hands should be washed afterwards. Although amphibian toxins do not usually affect healthy skin, some people are hypersensitive to them. The result is an allergic reaction, which may take a stormy course and endanger life. Here again, prompt medical aid is needed.

INDEX